American Macrobiotic Cuisine

American Macrobiotic Cuisine

by
Meredith McCarty

Turning Point Publications ☯

Published by: Turning Point Publications
1122 M Street
Eureka, California 95501

Library of Congress Cataloging-in-Publication Data

McCarty, Meredith, 1946-
   American macrobiotic cuisine.

   Includes index.
     1. Macrobiotic diet — Recipes.   2. Cookery, American.
I. Title
RM235.M38   1986   641.5'63   85-16481
ISBN 0-934947-02-3

Acknowledgments

Thanks to these friends for their help in getting me started and continuing to deepen my understanding of a truly natural way of health and happiness called macrobiotics.

My mother and father, Betty and Al James; my sister, Leone Webster; my husband, Patrick; my teachers, Aveline and Michio Kushi, Cornellia and Herman Aihara, Shizuko Yamamoto, Hiroshi Hayashi, Noboru Muramoto, Jacques and Yvette de Langre, Justine and Jeremiah Liebermann, Ken and Ann Burns, Susan and Duncan Sim; and friends Barbara Driscoll, Alice McGovern, Linda Wiesner, Sherman Goldman, Michael Wheeler, Lenny Jacobs, Anne Marie and Chris Erickson, Steve Miller, Melanie Ferreira, Martha Forbes, Monique and Paul Miksis, Irith and Larry Wieland, Holly and Mark Blackwood, Susanne Liberty and John Barger, Carolyn Real, Joan Frame, Linda Redfield, Alison Murray, Bob Wunner, and Denise Downey.

Thanks also to Harold Dagold for typing, Dianne Bitte for her help with the index, Susan Stearns for editing, Sandy Rothman for proofreading, Mari Kennedy for photographing the cover of the book, Pioneer Graphics of Eureka, California for their typography and camera-ready production, and Susan Reid for designing the Turning Point logo.

For permission to use drawings, thanks go to Dover Publications, Inc. for *Food and Drink: A Pictorial Archive from Nineteenth Century Sources*, selected by Jim Harter, Third Revised Edition, copyright 1983; and to W. Atlee Burpee Co. for *Burpee's Farm Annual for 1888*, copyright 1975.

Lastly, the East West Foundation, the *East West Journal, Macromuse, Macrobiotics Today*, the Arcata Co-op, and the Tofu Shop in Arcata, California have educated and inspired many toward greater health and happiness.

Contents

Table Seasonings 45

Vegetables from Land and Sea 49

Salads 61

Beans and Soyfoods 71

Introduction

American Macrobiotic Cuisine celebrates North America as a melting pot of cultures and their cuisines. The misconception that macrobiotics is an Oriental diet is gradually giving way to an understanding of its true nature as a most healthful, adaptable way of life for anyone.

Most of us have roots in more than one country. Our descendants came to North America for a new beginning—a better, freer life where their hopes and dreams could be realized. They settled in pockets, often according to nationality, and shared their common languages, foods, and customs. Over the decades and then centuries, the great ethnic differences softened and blended so that we now grow up experiencing many cultures from an early age.

I remember being raised in New York City and then on the edge of the Italian section of our Connecticut town. Italian food became a family favorite so much that spaghetti and meatballs and pizza were standard fare. It wasn't until I worked in New York at *Vogue Magazine* and in Boston as an office temporary and a potter that I came to appreciate the subtleties of Italy's luscious, multifaceted cuisine. French, Greek, and Chinese—and, more recently, early and Native American, Japanese, and Mexican—foods have added their delicious influences as well.

America's rich cultural heritage is fertile ground for the balancing of the traditional culinary wisdom of Occident and Orient with our new awareness of the importance of low-fat, high-fiber foods for a healthy, happy life. Indeed, the traditional staple foods of humanity—whole cereal grains, vegetables, beans, and fruits—may be prepared in an unending variety of ways if one takes the time to evaluate standard everyday food preparations and then upgrades the quality with the help of macrobiotic guidelines.

After studying macrobiotics in Boston for two years while on the staff at the *East West Journal*, I felt impelled to visit a traditional culture. Desiring to see a place where people still based their lives, diet, and agriculture on grains and vegetables, I chose the Yucatán in Mexico. The natives there are descendants of the ancient Mayans. It was a month-long experience that changed my life—and yes, they still do grow and enjoy corn, rice, black and other beans, and a variety of vegetables as their principal foods.

The other thing I needed to do was become more self-sufficient by learning to grow and cook natural foods in a country environment. The Still Mountain Society's summer program at their 250-acre macrobiotic homestead in the Canadian Rockies was my choice (R.R. #1, Fernie, B.C., Canada VOB 1MO). We gardened and took herb walks, cooked on woodstoves for thirty-five people, and I learned more about natural living than I could have hoped for.

On my return to Boston I met Patrick, my husband, in a shiatsu acupressure massage class at a macrobiotic seminar. Among other things, we shared our dreams of learning how to present macrobiotics to small-town North America. I moved to Eureka, California, to join Pat in this rather remote Pacific north coast community (immediate population 24,500) and in 1978 with our friend Steve Miller we incorporated as a nonprofit organization for natural health education—the East West Center for Macrobiotics.

Since that time we have served people through counseling sessions and classes in macrobiotic cooking and shiatsu massage. We serve weekly dinners at the Center covering themes ranging from everyday and regional American cooking and historic and festive meals to international gourmet macrobiotic cuisine, and recipes are provided for all the dishes.

At Steve's country place in Willow Creek, an hour's drive east of Eureka into the Coast Range mountains, we've hosted the annual Three Creeks Macrobiotic Summer Camps since 1978. During this week-long August program, over a hundred people study and enjoy many aspects of a healthy lifestyle, including various forms of exercise, meditation, shiatsu massage, good food, and a clean environment. The recipes in this book were all served at summer camp.

It has been my joy to research cuisines of the world and to transform certain ingredients and cooking techniques using the wisdom of macrobiotics. Even greater pleasure is derived from seeing people enjoy the meals. Their health improves and their understanding and appreciation of the natural way deepens along with our own.

A personal wish would be fulfilled if these recipes were used by individuals or small groups getting together to enjoy each other while expanding their culinary horizons or, on a larger scale, by institutions or restaurants.

M.M.

What Is Macrobiotic Cooking?

Macrobiotic cooking is distinguished from other forms of cooking by its holistic approach. The word "macrobiotics" means large view (macro) of life (biotics) compared with the microscopic view which sees the parts. Macrobiotics brings a depth of understanding to the kitchen as its practice cultivates a spirit or an attitude of appreciation and participation in the cycles of nature.

The idea of **principal foods** is very important in the macrobiotic approach. Foods which have sustained humanity since the use of fire and agriculture first began are those plants which the earth produces in the greatest abundance — whole cereal grains. These are proper human foods.

Another basic guideline in macrobiotic cooking is the selection and preparation of foods which are **in season** and are **grown as locally as possible**. Over time, this new approach brings awareness of the world around us and a feeling of harmony with natural order. By eating these foods we become acclimated to life in our area and as strong as the foods which survive well in the particular season.

I love best to have each thing in its season only, and enjoy doing without it at all other times.
    —Henry Thoreau, journal entry, December 5, 1856

Grains, beans, sea vegetables, seeds and nuts are the "keepers," foods which store well through several seasons. These can be obtained from a greater distance — although this is not ideal — than the more perishable fresh vegetables and fruits.

Thinking and acting seasonally and locally is **economical** and **ecological** as well. Food bills are cut by at least a third and often by half when staple foods are supplemented by seasonal vegetables and fruits. Doctor bills become minimal if not non-existent, and visits to the dentist are usually for maintenance rather than repairing new cavities.

The implications of this approach for the renewal and well-being of our country's people are far-reaching. Used on a broad scale, in institutions such as schools, hospitals, prisons, old age homes, mental health clinics, business cafeterias and for welfare recipients, food costs would be cut dramatically. As health improved, employees and students would miss fewer days of work or school and attention span and output would increase. Patients' health would improve and inmates' behavior would stabilize. These statements have been documented on a small scale in several places. With an educational program to accompany the alternative menus, people would learn why and how to prepare the foods themselves. Our institutions could serve their intended purpose of rehabilitation instead of containment or confinement.

Cook me some food and I'll eat for a day.
Teach me to cook and I'll eat for a lifetime.

To cook macrobiotically is to serve the physical, mental, emotional, and spiritual health of yourself, your family, and friends as integral parts of the larger whole. The saying "internal ecology determines external ecology" applies well here. Food is our direct link with the environment. The qualities of a person with a healthy body and a clear mind capable of seeing the whole view are reflected in the way we treat each other, whether in our families or on the political level of global community, or in the way we treat our global household, the Earth. This is the dream of macrobiotics. The macrobiotic slogan, One Peaceful World, hails back to the days when macrobiotics was a peace movement in Japan. From this movement came the common-sense realization that beyond, but through, food comes the strong and healthy, sane and happy humanity which lives within natural order.

People ask why, when local foods are encouraged, macrobiotic people use a few foods imported from Japan. The universal concepts of macrobiotics were introduced to this country by Japanese people, the Kushis on the East Coast and the Aiharas on the West Coast. Through their teachings we have come to respect the value of whole grains as the staple food and we have also learned about new foods of the highest quality such as miso, soy sauce, sea salt, *umeboshi* plums and other pickles, certain table seasonings and vegetables from land and sea. Their flavors and nutritional qualities are so excellent, it would be foolish not to incorporate them into a practical approach to health. Since their introduction in the early 1960s, many of these foods are now grown and produced in this country. In fact, even Japanese miso is made with American soybeans! Slowly but surely, these foods are becoming Americanized as have so many favorites from European countries, Asia, and Mexico.

Food Groups

The chapters in this book have been set up according to food groups with the understanding that you probably won't prepare entire menus, but are more likely to start with a soup, or a whole grain or vegetable dish, or a single dessert.

Getting to know the foods included in the macrobiotic approach to diet and health is made simple by visualizing them on your plate as portrayed in the following illustration. Calorie charts and scales for weighing out grams are unnecessary with this more realistic approach. The amounts and proportions are variable depending on the season, climate, and individual needs and preferences. Some people eat 50 percent grains right away, but others gradually move in this direction, with a greater proportion of vegetables, beans, and other foods.

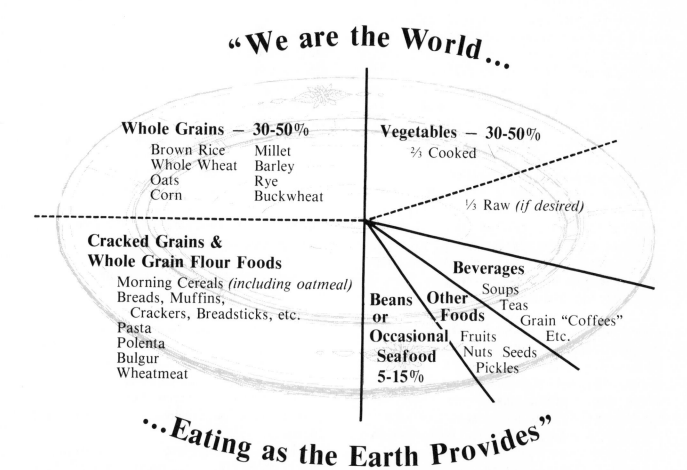

"We are the World...

Whole Grains — 30-50%

Brown Rice	Millet
Whole Wheat	Barley
Oats	Rye
Corn	Buckwheat

Vegetables — 30-50%

⅔ Cooked

⅓ Raw *(if desired)*

**Cracked Grains &
Whole Grain Flour Foods**

Morning Cereals *(including oatmeal)*
Breads, Muffins,
    Crackers, Breadsticks, etc.
Pasta
Polenta
Bulgur
Wheatmeat

Beverages
Soups
Teas
Grain "Coffees"
Etc.

Beans **Other**
or **Foods**
Occasional Fruits
Seafood Nuts Seeds
5-15% Pickles

...Eating as the Earth Provides"

Whole Grains

Whole grains are the main staple food in the macrobiotic approach to diet, comprising about 50 percent of food intake. They include the eight grains which are most widely available in the U.S.: rice, corn, wheat, millet, barley, rye, oats, and buckwheat. Most of the grain portion is served in the whole form, but at times some might be served cracked. Cracked grains include foods made from flour such as whole grain noodles, breads, and wheatmeat, and lightly processed grains such as rolled oats and bulgur. Whole grains contain all the nutrients, in perfect balance as created by nature, and are diminished somewhat by the oxidation that occurs with grinding. Of course, cracked grains by themselves are sometimes appropriate—for example, oatmeal for breakfast or a light meal of soup and whole grain bread.

There are several reasons why whole grains make up such a large portion of the diet. Grains grow in the greatest abundance of any food on the planet, and have always been the primary food source. Made up of complex carbohydrates, they are the ultimate energy source. When these complex sugars break down over time in our bodies into simpler sugars, we experience calm, sustained energy. This contrasts with the ups and downs which result from the simpler sugars found in sweets, fruit juice, and to a lesser extent in fruits. Simple sugars also occur in refined grain foods such as white flour products.

Known for the fiber and vitamin B in the bran layers, and the unsaturated oil containing vitamin E in the germ, whole grains are widely recognized to be rich in nutrients. In the July 1963 issue of *Scientific American*, professor Paul Mangelsdorf, Harvard University agronomist, wrote that "Cereal grains . . . represent a five-in-one food supply which contains carbohydrates, proteins, fats, minerals, and vitamins. A whole grain cereal, if its food values are not destroyed by the over-refinement of modern processing methods, comes closer than any other plant product to providing an adequate diet."

But this doesn't mean one could eat nothing but whole grains. Grains are completed and enhanced by the nutritional qualities and the flavors of other foods.

Land and Sea Vegetables

Land and sea vegetables are the second most important food category. A good variety of seasonal greens, roots, and squashes helps us to harmonize with the changing seasons. A little-known fact is that one could live without fruits, but not without vegetables. Vegetables contain all the nutrients fruits are praised for, and in greater amounts. Other surprising facts are that some greens contain more vitamin C than any fruit including oranges. Several green vegetables have more calcium than milk. High chlorophyll content is another valuable aspect of greens. Try to eat a minimum of two fresh vegetable dishes per day.

Sea vegetables are a renewable resource which stores and travels well. They've been enjoyed by people throughout history. Sea vegetables are the most highly mineralized foods on the planet, with hijiki leading the group. They are known for their detoxification properties as well as for being a source of vitamin B_{12}—not often found in a vegetarian diet, but known to exist in several foods included in the macrobiotic approach.

Most vegetables are served cooked, for greater digestibility, by a broad range of styles. Some vegetables are served raw for their light and cooling effects especially in summertime or when people have recently changed their focus from a meat, cheese, and egg-centered diet to one which focuses on grains and vegetables.

Beans and Soyfoods

The colorful variety of whole beans is well known, but soyfoods—good quality miso and soy sauce, tofu, and tempeh—are just now becoming popular on a broad scale. Beans are the main protein source in the macrobiotic way of eating. Grains contain a fair protein content, but are complemented by the protein in beans to form complete protein, a process which increases the amount of protein utilized by the body. This vegetable quality protein is as valuable as animal protein, without the cholesterol or saturated fats found in animal foods. Protein also occurs in nuts and seeds, but their high fat content (in the oil) renders them unsuitable as a main protein food.

Miso, a fermented soybean (and usually grain) paste, also contains vitamin B_{12} as well as bacteria similar to that in yogurt, due to fermentation. It is also a blood cleanser. The substance zybicolin attracts and expels from the body toxic substances such as radiation, pollution, and nicotine. Just small amounts of miso or soy sauce are used because of the salt content.

Tempeh is a valuable soyfood because it is made of whole soybeans which have been fully cooked and then fermented. On the other hand, tofu is just soymilk (without the soybean fiber) which has been coagulated. Because tofu is the more familiar soyfood for vegetarians, they sometimes eat it exclusively as a protein source because of its versatility and easy preparation. From the macrobiotic perspective, it is better to vary bean foods.

Only a small portion of beans is needed due to the nitrogen waste products which must be processed and excreted by the body. You don't need to prepare a pot of beans for every meal. Miso soups, or vegetables seasoned in the last few minutes of cooking with soy sauce, are suitable alternatives to meals which include a bean dish. Soy sauce is generally not served at the table; Americans often abuse it, thus oversalting their food.

The macrobiotic approach to cooking is not strictly vegetarian or vegan. Fish and shellfish are protein foods which are included occasionally. When eaten, they substitute for beans.

Beverages

Beverages include soups, non-stimulating teas, and cereal grain "coffees" taken after meals. Good quality alcoholic beverages are enjoyed on special occasions, if desired, and when one is in good health.

Fruits, Nuts, Seeds, and Pickles

The last food category includes fruits, nuts, seeds, and pickles. Fruits are often served as dessert, although other types of dessert would also go here. Fruits are chosen fresh in season like vegetables, or dried, and should be the kinds which would grow in your area.

Nuts and seeds and "butters" made from them are used in small quantities in desserts, or in spreads and sauces, or flavorful sprinklings for whole grains.

Just a few slices of pickle help to improve digestion and assimilation.

Why No Dairy?

You have probably noticed that dairy products and eggs have not been mentioned thus far. Cheese, butter, milk, ice cream and other dairy products are not usually included in the macrobiotic approach to diet for several reasons.

Cow's milk is the perfect food for a baby calf which will grow to weigh 2000 pounds. The enzymes and protein-carbohydrate ratio of cow's milk (3.8:4.5) differ greatly from human milk (1.5:6.0) which is the perfect human baby food (*The Macrobiotic Way of Natural Healing*, Michio Kushi, East West Publications, 1978). Once an infant is weaned, "milks" and then gruels made mostly from grains with lesser amounts of vegetables and beans are proper human foods. Many babies find animal milk hard to digest, or even intolerable.

Dairy products in general contain high amounts of fat which contribute to the diseases that plague our country today.

Most cows live dreadful lives as part of the nationwide practice of factory farming. Their feed is laced with chemicals and their living conditions are often no more than a small indoor pen. The quality of their health and lives is inseparable from the milk they produce. (For more specific information see the pamphlet *Factory Farming*, available from Friends of Animals, Inc., One Pine Street, Neptune, NJ 07753.)

Menu Planning

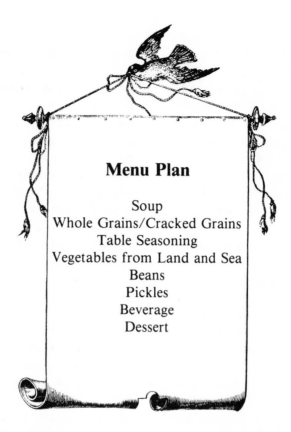

Menu Plan

Soup
Whole Grains/Cracked Grains
Table Seasoning
Vegetables from Land and Sea
Beans
Pickles
Beverage
Dessert

Everyday Menu Planning

Cooking class participants always ask if they need to cook all the food at every meal. It's easier than that! Breakfast may consist of a simple bowl of oatmeal, or whole wheat toast and tea, or one of the whole grain cereals in the breakfast section. Some people like to take their miso soup at breakfast time as they find it gives them a feeling of balanced alertness. Most others prefer soup with lunch or dinner.

The plate illustration (see page 5) serves as a guide for everyday whole meals, lunch and/or dinner. It may only be dinner for people who spend their days away from home, or lunch for people who eat their main meal of the day at that time. I usually prepare a full meal at lunchtime. Grains, and sometimes beans, are left to be reheated for dinner, so the only food I'll cook at that time is a vegetable dish.

The few minutes it takes to **visualize** a meal go far to create a balanced menu. Menu planning can be approached in two ways. In the first, you go over food groups in your head as you look around your kitchen to see what is already prepared and what foods you have on hand to cook. In the other approach, you actually write down your ideas for a complete meal, revising them as you go. Either way, macrobiotic cooking may be simple or more complex, depending on your capabilities, purpose, desire, and time.

Since **grains** are the main focus of every meal and often require the longest preparation, they should be prepared in a volume great enough to last several meals, unless you are willing to spend the time preparing them daily. Four cups of rice, pressure cooked with five to six cups of water and one-half teaspoon of sea salt, is the basic recipe I use. (Different batches of rice and pressure cooker brands call for varying amounts of water.) Cooked grains may be stored in the kitchen covered with a natural fiber cloth or mat, instead of in the refrigerator where the taste and texture are altered. If you must refrigerate them, be sure to reheat them before serving.

If you don't have cooked grain on hand, whole grain bread and noodles are quick alternatives.

Table seasonings are usually made once a week to be stored in a cool, dry, dark place like all other foods.

Vegetables are second in importance and should be prepared fresh at every meal. The easy vegetable cooking techniques in this book make for great variety. Be sure to include greens and roots every day. Always serve a lightly cooked vegetable dish at every meal. One dish might include both roots and greens such as sautéed onion, carrot, and kale. Two simple vegetable dishes might be served together such as lightly steamed or boiled greens with a sautéed or baked combination vegetable dish or a hearty vegetable stew.

Soups are another place to focus on vegetables from land and sea. Wakame, kombu, and nori sea vegetables cook up easily in soups along with land vegetables. For a really simple complete meal, prepare a soup or stew with a variety of vegetables and a prepared bean food, such as tempeh or tofu, to complement a grain dish.

Beans are not essential at every meal, but they should be included every day. Soak and cook two cups of dry beans once or twice a week. Alternate whole beans with tempeh or tofu which require little preparation and contribute to greater variety.

Pickles require only the time it takes to cut them if you buy good quality commercial varieties, or a little longer if you prepare your own. Their deep flavors and superior nutritional benefits make them appropriate to serve with both lunch and dinner.

Beverages include cereal grain "coffees" and herb or twig teas (and, of course, soup). Prepare a pot at a time and you have enough for several meals.

Creative Menu Planning

Although I didn't know how to boil water for noodles when I began macrobiotics twelve years ago, I now enjoy the challenge of creating gourmet meals according to the high standards of macrobiotics.

All menu planning is a creative endeavor, but festive, gourmet, or international menus are especially fun to research and plan. Ideas come from everywhere: travel at home and abroad, restaurant menus, cookbooks borrowed from a public library or from a friend, the recipes and beautiful pictures in women's magazines (I breeze through six months' worth during each visit with my mother-in-law!), or even from the labels on prepared food items. Historic information on the way people ate often shows up in novels or biographies. Natural foods restaurants are great places to see which dishes are most popular with the general public. The visual extravaganza *Entertaining*, by Martha Stewart (Clarkson N. Potter, Inc., New York, 1982), is a must for anyone interested in presenting food with grace, charm, and color. (Be creative in revising the ingredients.)

Macrobiotic food is to be enjoyed as we celebrate life, especially on special occasions when, in addition to maintaining health and preventing disease, we aim to entertain and satisfy. With practice you can create your own uncomplicated recipes for delicious, attractive dishes which have inspired you.

Upgrade recipe quality by converting ingredients and cutting down on unnecessary amounts of oil, sweetener, and seasoning. Soy sauce or dark or light miso bouillons or consommés substitute well for animal-based (beef or chicken) stocks. Tofu substitutes beautifully for dairy foods from cheese to whipped cream, but must always be fresh for the flavor and texture to be just right. Corn oil is the best butter replacement since it is the one most similar in texture and color. Wheatmeat is the perfect stand-in for meat or chicken.

When doing research, beware of recipes written today which attribute their source to native peoples, but which contain ingredients traditional people never ate—for example, sugar, margarine, baking soda and powder.

When creating more elaborate menus, **develop an eye for balance** in flavors, textures, and colors. A lightly seasoned or unseasoned dish combines well with a more heavily seasoned dish at the same meal. A delicate dish like steamed greens with carrot flowers counterbalances a stronger dish, say a brown rice and vegetable salad with an herb vinaigrette dressing or a chunky root vegetable stew. A dry dish harmonizes with another menu item which has a lot of sauce.

If one dish is **garnish**ed with minced green onion tops or chives, garnish another with a sprinkling of toasted seeds or a large sprig of parsley, watercress, or fresh herb. Or try bright orange thinly sliced carrot flowers or the edible flowers from nasturtiums, calendula (pot marigold), violets, borage, mustard, or kale.

Always **take into account the health of the people being served**. Examine all the recipes to be sure you haven't used oil or seasonings such as herbs, spices, garlic, or ginger, soy sauce, pickled plum *(ume)* vinegar, salt, or pepper in more than one or two dishes. I've omitted garlic in several recipes in the Mexican and Italian dinners because it appeared in other dishes at the same meal. This way each dish speaks for itself but is not masked by over-enhancement. I almost always serve rice in one form or another to satisfy people who enjoy it so much they come to expect it, and for others who are allergic to wheat, corn, and oats.

For people who are using daily food to regain their health, omit herbs and strong seasonings altogether. You'll be surprised by how beautiful and satisfying even "food as medicine" can be.

> *Let your food be as medicine*
> *and your medicine be food.*
> — Hippocrates

When choosing an **international** theme, you may want to select one of the most popular ethnic restaurant foods. At the present time in the U.S., Italian, Chinese, and Mexican restaurants are the favorites. Anytime we offer these themes for Thursday night dinners at the Center, more people than usual make reservations. Other international dinners we've served include Japanese, African, Merry Old English Fare, German Octoberfest, Irish, French, Greek, Russian, Moroccan, and Indian. Among the regional U.S. theme menus we've developed macrobiotically are Early American, Native American, Southern, and Texas Ranch House Cookin'.

And don't forget the extras for making the occasion really special — **flowers, candles, and music.** Fresh flowers add joy to any table setting in a very simple but colorful way. Candles add a cozy feeling of warmth and a glow during the fall and winter months. Music relaxes when it is played in the background, and stimulates the feeling for a good time. It's fun to choose ethnic music to accompany particular menu themes.

To serve large groups, from thirty upward, almost all of the recipes in this book convert well. Sometimes the liquid volume decreases as the solid proportions increase. For instance, four cups of rice may require six cups of water for pressure cooking, but six cups of rice only require seven cups of water.

Serving sizes are almost impossible to predict, although I have done so here. If you serve individual portions for the guests, you can plan ahead easily, but if you serve buffet style where the guests serve themselves, they will surprise you. If you have a particular dish they really like, it will be gone in a flash. So much for balanced, enlightened eating! Rice served with a gravy or sauce goes much faster than when it is served with a tasty but simpler table seasoning such as sesame salt. If you serve two grains at a meal, say a rice dish with whole grain bread, people will eat less rice and will gobble up the bread.

Also, a dish which served four for a simple three-item lunch at home may serve six when included as part of a more elaborate meal. At a dinner party or a summer camp, when people eat and drink leisurely while enjoying each other's company, all the food will most likely be eaten because there is time to really savor the experience and have second helpings or more.

Menus —————————————————————————

	SATURDAY	SUNDAY	MONDAY	TUESDAY
Breakfast		Indian Meal Cereal Roasted Corn Tea	Traditional Whole Oats with Dulse-Onion Sauce or Vegetable-Miso Seasoning *(Tekka)* Twig Tea	Cracked Wheat and Corn Cereal with Toasted Sunflower Seeds Resteamed Rice Alfalfa Tea
Lunch		Everyday Miso Soup Holly's Rice Salad with Herb Vinaigrette Dressing Sesame Salt Steamed Greens with Carrot Flowers Corn on the Cob with Pickled Plum *(Umeboshi)* Wild Nori Crackers Caraway Cabbage Pickles Red Clover Tea	Wheat Pilaf with Sesame Salt Baked Tempeh with Lemon-Mustard Sauce *Umeboshi* Cabbage Sea Palm Saute Pressed Vegetable Salad No. 1 Daikon and Carrot Miso Pickles Twig Tea	Leek-Soy Broth Soup Vegetable Millet with Sesame-Miso Powder Nutty Noodle Bake Arame-Broccoli Salad with Light Plum-Parsley Dressing Miso Carrot Tops Sauerkraut Salad Twig Tea
Dinner	Cream of Corn Soup with Dulse Watercress Rice with Shiitake Mushroom Sauce Sesame Breadsticks Seasonal Vegetable Saute Daikon Radish-Soy Sauce Mash Pickles Fresh Grape Gel with Nutty Granola Topping Twig Tea	*Chinese Dinner* Long Grain Brown Rice with Sesame-Nori Sprinkles Tofu Egg Foo Young Mung Bean Threads with Chinese Cabbage and Mushrooms Sweet and Sour Broccoli and Onions with Wheatmeat Quick Chinese Turnip Pickles Almond and Ginger Cookies Twig Tea	*Mexican Dinner* Tortilla Soup Mexican Rice with Sesame Salt Green Corn Tamale Bake Boiled Greens with Toasted Pumpkin Seeds Caramel Custard *(Flan)* Cinnamon and Regular Grain "Coffees"	*French Cuisine* French Onion Soup Short Grain Rice with Wild Rice and Rye Berries Sesame Salt Summer's Mixed Vegetable Quiche *Salade de Legumes avec Vinaigrette Bonne Femme* (Boiled Vegetable Salad with Housewife's Dressing) Poached Pears in Cherry Sauce Grain "Coffee"

WEDNESDAY	THURSDAY	FRIDAY	SATURDAY	SUNDAY
Irish Oatmeal with Dulse Sesame Salt Red Clover Tea	East Meets West Morning Cereal Sesame-Shiso Sprinkles Roasted Rice-Twig Tea	Cream of Wheat Roasted Sunflower Seeds Roasted Corn Tea		*Brunch* Buckwheat Noodles *(Soba)* in Light Ginger-Soy Broth Pearl Barley Rice with Sesame Salt Vegetable Saute with *Ume-Kuzu* Sauce Cucumber Aspic with Tofu Sour Cream Fresh Fruit Salad with Apple-Cinnamon Sauce Twig Tea
Japanese Cool Noodle Salad Whole Grain Breads and Rice Cakes with Chickpea Spread *(Hummus)* Composed Boiled Salad with *Ume* Vinegar Corn on the Cob	Green Onion Rice with Sesame Salt Sunshine Pie Boiled Onions and Mixed Greens with Sunflower Sprinkles Dulse-Sprout Salad with Lemon-Poppy Seed Dressing Red Radish *Ume* Pickles Roasted Rice-Twig Tea	Brown Rice with Wheat Berries Sesame-Nori Sprinkles Spiral Noodle Salad with Tofu Green Goddess Dressing Pressed Vegetable Salad No. 2 Cool Twig Tea	*Picnic* Journeycakes Rice Balls Corn on the Cob Nori-Nut Trail Mix Watermelon	
Japanese Cookery Vegetable Miso Soup Shaped Azuki Rice with Shiso Powder or Sesame-Nori Sprinkles Assorted Rice and Vegetable Rolls *(Sushi)* Cucumber-Wakame Salad Sesame Aspic *(Kanten)* Glazed Red Radishes Melon Slice with Berry-Fresh Mint Garnish Roasted Barley Tea *(Mugicha)*	*Native American Dinner* Hopi Stew Cracked Corn Rice with Toasted Pumpkin Seeds Pinto Beans and Hominy Summer's End Vegetable Dish Baked Indian Pudding Hominy Tea	*Italian Night* Minestrone Pasta Patricio Polenta Squares with Red Vegetable Sauce Steamed Kohlrabi Bulbs and Greens Lemon-Lime Pudding Pie Anise or Regular Grain "Coffees," Espresso style	*Early American Cooking** New England Boiled Dinner with Wheatmeat Rice with Sunflower-Sage Gravy Boston Baked Beans Blue and Yellow Cornmeal Muffins Dill Pickles American Berry Pie Alfalfa Tea *This menu appears in the cover photo.	

Easy Table of Measurements

All measurements are level unless otherwise stated.

3 teaspoons	=	1 tablespoon
¼ cup	=	4 tablespoons
½ cup	=	8 tablespoons
1 cup	=	16 tablespoons
2 cups	=	1 pint
4 cups	=	1 quart

Recipe ingredients are generally listed in the order used.

Breakfasts

For a constant source of energy and the clarity of thought needed to accomplish our goals for the new day, unsweetened whole grain breakfasts are best. Everyone likes hot cereals on cold mornings. Delicious year-round, these breakfasts have been enjoyed throughout the world. A simple bowl of oatmeal, sprinkled with toasted sunflower seeds or mild sesame salt and served with a cup of tea or grain "coffee," is enough for many people who don't want to spend much time in the kitchen first thing in the morning. Oatmeal is a standard American and European breakfast food that almost everyone already knows how to prepare. In fact, the dictionary defines the word "porridge" as "oatmeal boiled slowly in water until it thickens." The flakes sold in natural food stores take slightly longer to cook than instant versions.

For even quicker breakfasts, cooked rice can be reheated by steaming or, as is done in Japan, hot tea may be poured over cooked rice from the night before. Hot soup poured over rice is very tasty as well. At camp, reheated rice is served as an alternative to the cereal. At home, I often mix cooked rice or other grains into morning cereal for added texture and variety— no further water is needed. Of course, whole grain bread, either steamed for about two minutes (the texture becomes cakelike) or lightly toasted, is another quick but satisfying breakfast food. Store-bought puffed-grain cereals or crumbled, unsalted rice cakes, served with soy, seed, or nut "milks," are easy-to-prepare breakfast foods which may also be enjoyed on occasion.

Since the high-fat, animal quality breakfast foods—bacon, eggs, and sausage—are already out of the picture, the other adjustment to be made is away from the habit of adding milk and sugar or honey to morning cereal. Sugar (and coffee) may give a quick surge of energy, but it is short-lived and lets you down before lunch. As your energy level decreases, you may be left feeling tired and discouraged. Of course, attempting to compensate mid-morning with a highly sugared snack or more coffee only makes you feel worse.

During a period of transition and on occasion, the addition of seasonal fruit, raisins, or a good quality sweetener changes the day's beginning from overly-sweet to more neutral and strengthening. Good quality sweeteners are syrups made from a variety of malted grains, including brown rice. Pure maple syrup is used less often for a sweeter flavor.

Morning cereals are made with the full spectrum of whole grains which are lightly or coarsely ground into flour or flakes. Ground grains, properly cooked alone or in combination, are easy to digest. The best quality flours are fresh-ground from organically grown grain. You may find that you want to purchase a hand or electric stone mill after you experience the superior flavor of fresh-ground flour. The nutrients in whole grains oxidize when the grains are ground. Up to 50% are lost within three days after grinding. For variety and ease in grinding, you may choose to toast the whole grain, flakes, or flour lightly before making cereal. One cup grain yields about 1½ cups flour. At any rate, store-bought whole grain flour is widely available and its slightly finer texture gives a very smooth, creamy texture to cereals as well as baked goods.

Flour is best soaked before cooking to thoroughly soften the hard particles. Overnight soaking makes for minimal preparation time in the morning and for a very creamy texture. However, if you forget to plan ahead, don't let it keep you from making these delicious cereals.

Cereals do need to be stirred until they come to a boil. In Iceland, cereal is appropriately known as "stirabout." Then they can be covered, flame spreader put underneath the pot, and left to cook over low heat for 15 minutes to ½ hour. The flame spreader (available at hardware stores) keeps the bottom from burning as do heavier pots made from stainless steel or cast iron. The B vitamins are preserved by keeping the grains away from direct heat. A flat-bottomed wooden spoon keeps cereal from settling on the bottom. A wire whisk is a great help for smoothing out any lumps which occur when the water is added all at once instead of gradually forming a paste. To clean pots, simply soak in water until cereal stuck to bottom lifts off easily.

One cup of dry cereal usually serves two. The ratio of flour or flakes to water is usually 1:3 for flour or 1:2 for flakes. This ratio decreases for large volumes. Plan on 1 flour:2½ water or 1 flakes:1½ water for large amounts of cereal. For 70 people, 45 cups of flour to 112 cups water (or 11 quarts:28 quarts) to 2 tablespoons sea salt worked well. For flaked cereals to serve 60, 40 cups flakes:80 cups water (or 10 quarts:20 quarts):1½ tablespoons sea salt was a good estimate. Both times, no rice was served (which would have reduced the need for as much cereal).

The recipes which follow are nourishing and easy to prepare. Since tastes differ, try them and then decide if you'd like the texture to be wetter, drier, or just the way it is.

Breakfast Menu Plan

Cereal
Table Seasoning
Tea or Grain "Coffee"

Cream of Wheat

Serves 2
Makes a little less than 3 cups

Known to some as Bear Mush, this breakfast standard has a wonderful sweet flavor.

Notice that the ratio of flour to water is 1:3, and for all amounts above two cups flour, the amount of water decreases to 1:2½, or 2 cups flour:5 cups water. This general rule applies to all the flour-based cereals which follow.

1 cup whole wheat flour
3 cups water
⅛ teaspoon sea salt

Serves 4
Makes a little more than 5½ cups

2 cups whole wheat flour
5 cups water
¼ teaspoon sea salt

To prepare, soak flour overnight in cooking pot. In the morning, add salt and bring ingredients to boil over medium-high heat, stirring often to avoid sticking or lumping. Turn flame to medium-low, and cook covered for 15 minutes.

For cereal which has not been pre-soaked, cook for one-half hour over a flame spreader.

For large amounts, soak flour in enough of the measured water to cover. In the morning bring the remaining water to boil with the salt, and then add the soaked cereal and proceed as usual. This method saves time and effort spent waiting for a large volume of cereal to come to a boil while constantly stirring. It also lessens the chance of the cereal burning at the bottom of the pot.

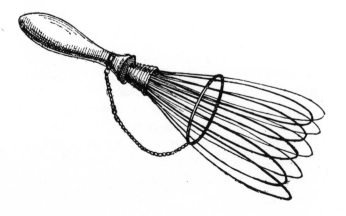

Cracked Wheat & Corn Cereal

Serves 2

Cracked wheat is whole wheat berries that have been coarsely ground and sifted. If you crack your own wheat, leave the flour in for a creamier cereal texture.

½ cup cracked wheat
½ cup cornmeal
3 cups water
⅛ teaspoon sea salt

To prepare, follow preceding *Cream of Wheat* directions.

East Meets West Morning Cereal

Serves 2

Thanks to an *East West Journal Cooklet*, now out of print, for this cereal idea.

⅔ cup brown rice flour
⅓ cup corn flour
3 cups water
⅛ teaspoon sea salt

To prepare, follow preceding *Cream of Wheat* directions.

Indian Meal

Serves 2

This is the first hot morning cereal I tasted when I began macrobiotics. Prepared from a package put out by Boston's pioneer macrobiotic-natural foods store, Erewhon, the remembrance of its unique flavor and smooth/crunchy texture led me to make it at home.

1 cup corn flour or meal
3 cups water
⅛ teaspoon sea salt
2 tablespoons sunflower seeds, toasted
2 tablespoons pumpkin seeds, toasted
1 tablespoon chia seeds (optional)

To prepare, follow preceding *Cream of Wheat* directions, adding seeds just before cooking.

Irish Oatmeal with Dulse

Serves 2-3

Dulse goes well with oats, taste-wise and historically, as both were prepared in Scotland and Ireland.

  1 cup whole oats, coarsely ground, or
      steel cut oats
  3 cups water
  ¼ cup dry dulse sea vegetable,
      loosely packed

One cup whole oats yields about 1⅓ cups coarsely ground meal. Prepare by following *Cream of Wheat* directions on preceding page.

    In the morning, soak dulse in water to cover until reconstituted, about one minute, then swish to release any particles of sand, squeeze and tear into pieces. Add to pot to cook. Use the soak water in another dish such as soup. Discard the very bottom portion where particles may settle.

Oatmeal

Serves 1-2
Makes 2 cups

Use oat flakes instead of quick cooking oats for the best flavor and toast them to enhance or revive the flavor only if you feel it's needed. Quick cooking oats which are often served in fast food restaurants tend to have a bland taste like the box they come in.

    Notice the ratio of flakes to water is 1:2 and for all amounts above two cups rolled oats, the amount of water decreases to 1:1½ or two cups flakes to three cups water.

  1 cup oat flakes (or rolled wheat, rye, or
      barley)
  2 cups water
  ⅛ teaspoon sea salt

Serves 2-3
Makes 3½ cups

  2 cups oat flakes (or rolled wheat, rye, or
      barley)
  3 cups water
  ¼ teaspoon sea salt

Flaked cereals don't need to be pre-soaked. Simply bring ingredients to boil, then turn heat low, and cover to cook for 15 minutes. When using a small pot, keep the lid ajar to prevent oats from foaming over.

    Add cooked whole grains to oatmeal for variety. No extra liquid is needed.

Traditional Whole Oats

Serves 3
Makes 4¼ cups

The creamiest cereal—it's so satisfying you won't believe you've waited so long to taste the richer flavor of whole grain oats. We call this cereal "traditional" because the oats are prepared the way they were before oat flakes were developed. Cooked in the old-timey way, overnight while you sleep, this hearty cereal is ready when you rise.

    See *Dulse-Onion Sauce* recipe (page 80) as topping for whole oats. Vegetable-Miso Sprinkles (*Tekka*, see page 45) also accent whole oats well.

  1 cup whole oat grains
  4 cups water
  ⅛ teaspoon sea salt

Before going to bed, rinse whole oats, then place in heavy cooking pot with water and salt. Bring to boil, then turn flame low, place flame spreader under pot, and cover to cook overnight. Stir well for smooth consistency when you arise.

    The long, slow flame uses no more energy than other cooking techniques, and definitely has a more nurturing feeling to it than quicker cooking.

Soups, Broths, and Stews

In the rural areas of France, *la soupe* has been the name of the evening meal for hundreds of years. This is where we get our word "supper." The word soup comes from the Latin "suppa" and is translated to swallow. In Sanskrit it is derived from *su* meaning good and *po* meaning to nourish. Traditionally, many people ate soups as hearty one-dish meals. As people became more "cultured," they stopped eating this "peasant" food. Today soups have become popular again.

Soup warms the body, causing good blood circulation. A study reported in the *Journal of the American Dietetic Association* found that people ate less when they made soup a regular part of lunches or dinners. Researchers also found that the more often people ate soup, the more excess weight they lost. One reason for this is that soup is hot and goes down only a spoonful at a time, so it takes time to eat.

Macrobiotic soups are based on grains, beans, and/or vegetables. They are usually flavored with fermented soybean paste (miso) or sometimes with good quality soy sauce, much as other cooks use beef or chicken bouillon. However, miso and soy sauce offer incredible nutritional qualities in addition to their richly delicious flavors (see page 73). Miso and soy sauce stimulate the taste buds and digestive juices, so soup seasoned with them prepares the body for the digestion of grain and other dishes which follow. Kombu sea vegetable added to soups also causes digestive action because of the glutamic acid which occurs naturally in kombu, instead of the chemical variety called MSG (monosodium glutamate) which is high in sodium.

The general rule I follow for amounts is 1 tablespoon of either miso or soy sauce per cup of water. This amount makes for very attractive flavors and has proved very satisfying for the groups I've served. However, the amount you use depends on your particular condition. Try the recipes as they stand, then revise them according to your tastes and needs. If you are very thirsty after a meal, you may need to cut down since miso and soy sauce do contain salt.

One serving of soup a day is usually enough for most people. Some do crave two servings a day, perhaps because of the minerals and other healing properties in sea vegetables and miso. Because we begin and end meals with liquid, we usually don't drink during the meal, when digestive juices are doing their work.

Simple meals are created when soup is served with a whole grain dish or bread. Cooked seasonal vegetables or a salad add variety; to expand your horizons even further, and when time allows, you can prepare the whole menus featured in this book. Better still, substitute miso or soy sauce for salt or other seasonings such as bouillon cubes in your own favorite soups.

For large groups, it works out perfectly to simply multiply soup ingredients. For example, if a recipe serves six and you want to serve sixty, multiply each ingredient by ten.

Everyday Miso Soup

Serves 5

This classic recipe includes ingredients which are so harmonious and healthgiving that people return to it time and time again. As you can see, much variation is possible, so be creative and use what you have on hand.

  4 cups water
  6 inch piece wakame sea vegetable
  ¼ cup onion (globe, leek, or green)
  ¼ cup carrot or other root vegetable
  ¼ cup daikon white radish
  ¼ cup seasonal green vegetable or
      wild greens, well packed
  ½ inch slice tofu, cubed (optional)
  ¼ cup barley *(mugi)* or other miso, or
      a combination of two kinds

Place sea vegetable and water in soup pot and bring to boil. Simmer while you cut the vegetables to similar size and shape. Remove sea vegetable, cool briefly and cut. Reserve midrib for another dish if it is too hard to chop fine for use in soup now. Return chopped sea vegetable to pot.

    Add all ingredients to soup pot except green onion tops (if used) and miso and slow boil until done, up to one-half hour, depending on how vegetables are cut. Traditionally, soup vegetables are well cooked so they melt in your mouth. A side dish of vegetables may be more lightly cooked.

    Dilute miso in a little of the hot soup liquid and add with green onion tops during the last three minutes of gentle simmering. It's important not to cook the miso at a rolling boil (which would kill the beneficial bacteria) but the miso should be well blended with the soup before serving.

    An alternative method is to add the dissolved miso to the soup, turn the heat off, and let it steep for 5-10 minutes before serving.

Vegetable Miso Soup

This simple miso soup was made on the spur of the moment with leftover ingredients that were used for flavor, but not served, in the *Sesame Aspic* from the Japanese dinner (see page 69). Other vegetables may substitute for the squash and carrot.

  Water to consistency desired
  Kombu from aspic, sliced thin
  Shiitake mushrooms from aspic, stems
    discarded and tops sliced thin
  Yellow summer squash, cut in thin rounds
  Carrot flowers, sliced thin
1 tablespoon miso per cup water
  Sunflower sprouts for garnish

Bring all ingredients, except miso and garnish, to boil, then turn heat low to simmer covered until done, about 10 minutes. Dissolve miso in a little of the hot soup stock and add to soup to simmer very gently during last three minutes of cooking. Garnish to serve.

French Onion Soup

Serves 8

1 tablespoon corn oil
4 cups onions, sliced
4 cups water
3 tablespoons soybean *(hatcho)* miso
8 slices whole wheat French bread or 1 cup croutons

Heat oil in pot. Add onions and sauté until slightly soft. Add water and bring to boil. Reduce heat and simmer one-half hour. Dilute miso in a little of the broth in a separate bowl, then add back to soup. Simmer gently three minutes before serving. Float a slice of bread or a small handful of croutons on top of soup to serve.

Minestrone

Serves 4

Vary the vegetables according to season. Summer squash is a nice addition during the warm months. With a small amount of beans such as this, it isn't necessary to presoak them.

¼ cup small white navy beans
5 cups water (2 cups to cook beans, 3 cups more for soup)
3 inch piece kombu sea vegetable
2 cloves garlic, minced
½ cup each carrot, cabbage, celery, and green onions, diced small
½ cup whole wheat shells or elbow macaroni
3 tablespoons barley *(mugi)* miso
2 tablespoons parsley, chopped

Bring beans to boil in two cups water in open pressure cooker and boil vigorously for five minutes. Add sea vegetable, cover, and bring to pressure to cook one-half hour. Remove sea vegetable from pot and dice. Return to soup with three cups more water, pasta, and vegetables (except parsley), return soup to boil, and slow boil until done, about 15 minutes.

Dissolve miso in a little of the hot soup broth and add to soup with parsley. Cook three minutes more over very low flame to blend flavors.

Tortilla Soup

Serves 4

¼ cup kidney beans
5 cups water (2 cups to cook beans,
    3 cups more for soup)
3 inch piece kombu sea vegetable
1 bay leaf
1 clove garlic, minced
1 small onion, diced
1 small carrot, diced
½ stalk celery, diced
2 corn tortillas
¼ cup parsley, chopped
3 tablespoons barley *(mugi)* miso

Bring beans to boil in two cups water in open pressure cooker and boil vigorously for five minutes. Add sea vegetable and bay leaf, cover, and bring to pressure to cook one-half hour. Cut tortillas in quarters crosswise, then across in half-inch strips.

Remove sea vegetable from pot and dice. Return to soup with three cups more water and the vegetables, resume boiling soup, and slow boil until done, about 15 minutes.

Dissolve miso in a little of the hot soup broth and add to soup with tortillas and parsley. Simmer very gently three minutes and serve.

Leek-Soy Broth Soup

Serves 3-4

A lovely soup, one of my favorites, rich and flavorful!

1 cup leek, sliced in ½ inch diagonals
4 cups (1 quart) water
6 inch piece kombu sea vegetable
6 dried *shiitake* mushrooms
3 tablespoons good quality soy sauce

Slice leek down center in order to separate and clean leaves before cutting. Keep white and green parts separate.

Place all ingredients except green part of leek and soy sauce in soup pot. Pre-soaking the mushrooms is not necessary. Bring to boil, then simmer until mushrooms are soft—about 15 minutes. Remove kombu and mushrooms. Set aside

kombu for use in another dish. Cut off and discard tough mushroom stems, slice tops and return to soup with leek greens and soy sauce. Simmer several minutes to cook leek greens and blend flavors.

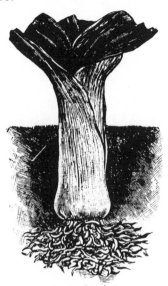

Cream of Corn Soup with Dulse

Serves 7

A hearty soup with a thick and creamy texture from the rolled oats. To enhance flavor, lightly toast oats by stirring them in a dry skillet over medium heat until barely golden and aromatic.

1 cup rolled oats
¼ cup dried dulse sea vegetable
1 small onion, sliced in thin crescents
1 ear corn (kernels)
1 stalk celery, cut in thin diagonals
½ medium rutabaga, quartered and cut
    crosswise in thin slices
5 cups water
6 tablespoons light miso
2 teaspoons celery and parsley leaves,
    minced for garnish

Place all ingredients, except miso and garnish, in soup pot and bring to boil. Turn flame to medium-low so soup simmers for one-half hour. If oats cause foaming, place flame spreader under pot and keep lid ajar. Dissolve miso in a little of the hot soup and add to pot to simmer very gently in last three minutes. Garnish to serve.

Buckwheat Noodles (Soba) in Light Ginger-Soy Broth

Serves 3 generously
Makes 3½ cups noodles

Noodles:

7 ounce package buckwheat noodles *(soba)*
6 cups water (1½ quarts)

Broth:

3 cups water
6 flower-cut carrots, thinly sliced
3 tablespoons good quality soy sauce
6 snow peas or 1 green onion top,
    cut in 1½″ slices
½ teaspoon ginger, fresh grated

To cook noodles, bring water to boil, then add noodles. Cook uncovered at a low boil until done, about 12 minutes. Drain, and if serving later, rinse under cool water to stop cooking.

To prepare broth, bring water and carrots to boil and simmer until carrots are soft, about five minutes. Add remaining ingredients and simmer two minutes more. Pour over noodles in individual soup bowls.

For a heartier broth, add up to 3 tablespoons more soy sauce.

For large amounts, steam carrots and peas or green onions separately and place two of each on top of individual servings, so they don't get lost in the pot.

Hopi Stew

Serves 6

Juanita Tiger Kavena, teacher for 32 years on the Hopi Reservation and married to a Hopi, has written a very inspiring cookbook, *Hopi Cookery* (The University of Arizona Press, Tucson, Arizona, 1980). Her book is a resourceful guide to a culinary tradition steeped in peace and harmony with the environment.

Wheatmeat substitutes for venison and the herbs substitute for the native varieties used in Hopi cooking.

Both wheatmeat cooking broth and a little sea salt are included in this recipe because a larger amount of the soy sauce-flavored broth alone makes the stew too dark.

1 onion
1 carrot
1 turnip
2 celery stalks or 2 large leafy greens
    (collard, turnip, etc.)
1 cup wheatmeat (see page 40)
2 tablespoons wheatmeat cooking broth or
    1 tablespoon good quality soy sauce
2 teaspoons dried sage and/or thyme; or
    1 tablespoon fresh, minced
4 cups water
½ teaspoon sea salt
12 *Cornmeal Dumplings*

Cornmeal Dumplings:

Makes about 12

1 cup blue or yellow cornmeal or corn flour
1½-1 cup water (less for cornmeal, more for
    corn flour)
⅛ teaspoon sea salt

To make dumplings, bring water and salt to boil and add to cornmeal. Boiling water softens the meal and makes for a more cohesive dough. Mix well. Form into one-inch balls with moistened hands, and flatten.

Cut vegetables and wheatmeat into one-inch chunks.

Place all ingredients, except dumplings and greens, in pot and bring to boil. Add dumplings and turn flame down to simmer one-half hour. Add greens in last 15 minutes of cooking time.

Whole Grains

Whole grains have always fed more people around the world than any other food, and still do. According to *The Oxford Book of Food Plants* (Masefield, Wallis, Harrison and Nicholson: Oxford University Press, 1969, London), from which much of this information about grains derives, "grain crops are by far the most important sources of plant food for man . . . the vast majority of mankind has always relied on a cereal as the basic staple of diet, with wheat and rice, and in America maize (corn), as the most important examples." And Professor Manglesdorf, Harvard University agronomist, says, "No civilization worthy of the name has ever been founded on any agricultural basis other than (whole grain) cereals."

The origin of many of the grains is uncertain, but their wild ancestors were probably the first crops that Stone Age man brought into cultivation. Grains are the storehouses of food for the young plant and consist mainly of carbohydrate (starch) with some protein, and traces of minerals and vitamins.

Rice, wheat, corn, oats, rye, barley, millet, and buckwheat are proper human foods because of their ecological nature—they grow in the greatest abundance of any food source on our planet, and they impart the most food energy from the least amount of land.

Energy is what everyone is looking for. The ability to visualize and to complete cycles is one element of a successful life. Since we eat to live, food is an unavoidable part of the process. Our choice in foods spells the difference between confusion, fear, lack of confidence, and depression—and the clarity, courage, will, and humor it takes to see a project through to its conclusion. The "project" might be anything from the paper that must be written for a class to a rela-

tionship which must be approached and resolved.

The **complex carbohydrates** in whole cereal grains give sustained energy over time. Complex carbohydrates are really complex sugars which break down slowly in the body, meanwhile generating energy to fulfill our dreams for the day, or a lifetime.

Fiber and bran are popular terms these days. What a perfect package whole grains are, balanced by nature so that fiber comes along with other nutrients. And how economical and ecological they are when compared with the processed bran and germ which is sold in cardboard boxes and glass jars. Who could ever add the right amount of rice polishings, or wheat germ and bran, to refined flour and come up with a suitable substitute for nature's wisdom?

The fiber in whole grains keeps the colon cleansed on a meal-to-meal basis. According to a study at McGill University in Montreal, Canada, brown rice reduces radiation absorbed by the intestines by 50-80 percent. The bran and germ are full of vitamins B and E respectively. Whole grains contain a good protein and iron content too. Ultimately, whole grains taste good when properly prepared. Their clean, satisfying flavors lend themselves to embellishment by tasty toppings from table seasonings to sauces and gravies.

Rice

Rice is one of the world's two most important food crops, the other being wheat. It originated in Asia and was already a staple food in China in 2800 B.C., and in India almost as early. Rice is grown from the equator to as far north as Japan. In Europe, where Italy has long been the leading producer, it has recently pushed further north, especially in southern France and Hungary. Rice is grown either in standing water or on dry land like any other grain. The U.S. is now the world's largest rice exporter.

In parts of Asia where the major portion of the diet consists of polished or white rice, a disease called "beriberi" used to be prevalent. It is caused by deficiency of vitamin B_1 (thiamine) which is present in the bran and germ but not in the center of the grain.

There are only three commercial organic rice growers in the U.S. We can support their good efforts and our personal health by choosing organic rice when we shop.

There are four kinds of brown rice available—short, medium, and long grain, and sweet rices. Short grain is used most often in a temperate climate for its delicious flavor and the strength it imparts. Long grain rice is especially nice for people who expect all rice to have the light and fluffy texture of white rice. It's a good summertime grain as well. (Basmati rice is a type of long grain rice from India which is becoming popular in this country. It's known for its fragrance.) The texture of medium grain rice resembles short more than long grain rice. Sweet brown rice should really be called sticky rice, since it is a variety of short grain which contains a high portion of gluten. It may be cooked along with regular short grain rice. Traditionally in Japan it is cooked and then pounded into a sticky mass and shaped into balls called *mochi*. There are no recipes for sweet rice in this cookbook.

Wild rice is the only grain native to North America. It is actually a tall aquatic grass.

How to Cook Rice

There are so many ways to prepare brown rice, from the simplest daily fare of *Basic Brown Rice*, with its many easy variations, to more fancy pilafs which are suitable for special occasions. See *Holly's Rice Salad* recipe (page 62) for a rich-tasting brown rice dish which will satisfy anyone. Cooking rice uses less energy and takes less work than making bread.

Pressure cooked short grain brown rice is often preferred for its soft, perfect texture. If you've experienced gummy, watery, or hard rice, try this method. Pressure cooking also seals in all the nutrients. By all means, learn to use a pressure cooker for the best tasting and most digestible grains and beans. Do not pressure cook long grain rice, however. Boiling it with one and a half times as much water as rice makes for light long grain rice. Directions for pressure cooked or boiled short grain brown rice and for boiled long grain rice follow.

Rinse rice by placing it in cooking pot with water to cover about two inches above rice. Even if the rice is clean after milling, some dust occurs because the rice is stored in big bags and moved around during transportation, causing the kernels to scrape against each other. Stir with your hand in an orderly, circular motion several times. Stop and see the small particles which rise to the surface or turn the water murky. Pour water off through strainer to be sure to catch any rice kernels. Do this one to three times, until water is clear, and do it quickly so nutrients don't leach into the water only to be thrown away. Return rinsed rice to pressure cooker or other pot.

There are two methods for determining the proper amount of **water** to add to cook rice. The first is a general rule of one-and-a-quarter to one-and-a-half times the amount of rice for pressure cooking (depending on the kind of cooker) or one-and-a-half to two times the amount of rice for pot cooking. The amount of water decreases as the amount of rice increases. Six cups of rice calls for seven cups water for pressure cooking.

The other technique liberates one from the measuring cup. It's called **The Finger Method** and can be used for amounts over four cups.

Place rinsed rice in pressure cooker or pot and add water. Make rice level by smoothing with your hand; place your middle fingertip on top of rice. Measure water to within first and second joint from fingertip. Water to the first joint yields drier rice than rice cooked with water up to the second joint. Try this method and see which kind of rice you and your family or friends prefer. For babies and for old or sick people, make grain softer by increasing water and cooking time.

From experience we have determined these amounts. Here, the space between finger joints is estimated to be one inch long.

For four cups rice, water level reaches a little above the first joint (1¼ inches) above rice — 5-6 cups water.

For six cups rice, water level reaches one-and-a-half joints (1½ inches) above rice — 7-8 cups water.

For eight cups rice, water level reaches two joints (two inches) above rice — 9 cups water.

For ten cups rice, water level reaches two-and-a-half joints (2½ inches) above rice — about 9½ cups water.

For twelve to thirty cups rice, water level reaches three joints (three inches) above rice.

At this point you may want to get into the habit of **soaking** short grain brown rice before cooking. Anytime from an hour to overnight helps to make the grains even more tender, and the nutrients more available as the B vitamins go into the water.

For rice with a flakier texture, add boiling salted water to rice and boil, or toast rice in a skillet until it turns a light golden color before cooking.

Good quality sea **salt** is added to rice (and other grain) to make it more digestible. Salt helps break down the rice, and through chemical combination renders it more alkaline when cooked. Figure one-eighth teaspoon sea salt per cup dry rice. This is the minimum you'll find recommended anywhere. As a basis of comparison, notice the amount on supermarket rice directions, one teaspoon per cup. After eating grains and vegetables for several years, as your backlog of excess salt is depleted, you may choose to use a little more salt, perhaps one quarter teaspoon per cup dry grain.

Cover pot and bring to **pressure or boil.** When grain reaches pressure or boiling point, turn flame low and place flame spreader (also called a heat deflector or diffuser, available at hardware stores) under the pot. Cook undisturbed (do not stir rice) for one hour, or at least 45 minutes, in pressure cooker. You should always be able to hear the gentle hiss of the pressure cooker which tells you the pressure is still up.

Let the pressure come down naturally after turning off flame or, if you are in a hurry, place pressure cooker under cool running water until air vent collapses, indicating the pressure has subsided.

To serve, gently spoon grain into serving bowl so grains are light, and not hard-packed. Enjoy with a table seasoning or condiment sprinkled over the grain, or with a sauce or gravy. To complete the dish, garnish with chopped fresh greens such as parsley, green onions, or chives.

Store cooked rice in a wooden or pottery serving bowl covered with a natural fiber cloth or mat. Since refrigerating rice alters its natural good taste and texture, keep it in a cool part of your kitchen. If the climate is quite hot and you do store cooked rice in the refrigerator, steam it before eating. Cook rice daily if you don't want to use reheated rice or don't have a refrigerator in hot seasons.

To reheat rice, spoon into a steamer basket or add to a saucepan with a small amount of water in the bottom, or sauté with vegetables. Ready in minutes.

Figuring amounts for large groups is never certain, but here are some estimates. People always eat more pressure cooked short grain brown rice than boiled short or long grain rice. Plan one-quarter cup dry rice per person for newcomers, one-third to one-half cup when you are also serving a cracked grain dish such as bread, pasta, or wheatmeat, and one-half to one cup per serving for rice eaters. At camp, thirty-five cups short grain brown rice, boiled, served seventy people. Two-and-a-half cups dry rice weighs one pound.

The recipes in this book start with two cups of dry grain because many people feel they won't use more than that amount. However, try cooking four cups dry rice at a time so you have enough to last for three days. Recipes for both two cups and four cups dry rice are listed here.

Happiness is the ultimate goal.
Don't substitute brown rice for happiness.
—Herman Aihara

Basic Short Grain Brown Rice

Serves 4-6
Makes 5-6 cups

2 cups brown rice, organic short grain
¼ teaspoon sea salt
2½-4 cups water (2½-3 cups for pressure cooking, 4 cups for boiling)

Serves 8-12
Makes 10-11 cups

4 cups brown rice, organic short grain
½ teaspoon sea salt
5-6 cups water for pressure cooking or boiling

Rinse rice, drain, and place in pressure cooker or other cooking pot with water and salt. Cover and bring to pressure or boil. Turn heat to medium-low, place flame spreader under pot, and cook for one hour. See detailed descripton on pages 26 and 27.

Variations: One good way to experience all the grains and still enjoy the favorite, brown rice, is to substitute a small amount of any other grain for part of the rice in cooking. Try the following recipes for a broad range of ways to enjoy brown rice, and then experiment on your own adding millet, whole oats, or bulgur to rice.

Brown Rice with Wheat Berries

Prepare as usual, but substitute two tablespoons wheat berries (hard or soft wheat) for same amount of rice in the *Basic Short Grain Brown Rice* recipe above. Pressure cook to completely soften wheat.

Rice with Wild Rice and Rye Berries

Serves 4-6

1¾ short or long grain brown rice
2 tablespoons wild rice
2 tablespoons rye berries

Prepare according to preceding *Basic Short Grain Brown Rice* recipe. For directions on cooking long grain brown rice, see page 32.

Pearl Barley Rice

Pearl barley (called *hato mugi* in Japanese) is more like a wild grass than a grain. It is highly revered by Oriental people. According to Chinese medicine, pearl barley is believed to dispel heat and dissolve tumors in the body. The Japanese traditionally stretched their favorite grain, rice, by cooking it with barley. Buy pearl barley in Oriental food stores. In contrast to American pearl*ed* barley, pearl barley has not been stripped of its bran layers. Everyone will enjoy it prepared this way.

1½ cups short grain brown rice
½ cup pearl barley

Clean pearl barley by spreading it out on a plate as for beans. Discard any hulls or foreign matter, then rinse as usual along with rice. Prepare according to preceding *Basic Short Grain Brown Rice* recipe.

Cracked Corn Rice

Serves 4-6

1½ cups short grain brown rice
½ cup cracked corn

To crack corn, rinse whole kernels, then toast in a skillet, stirring often, until dry and slightly golden in color. The aroma is wonderful! Crack by grinding on an open setting of a hand or electric mill. Sift out flour for a more distinct texture. One cup whole corn yields 1¼ cups cracked and sifted.

Prepare according to preceding *Basic Short Grain Brown Rice* recipe, using pressure cooking technique to thoroughly soften the corn.

Delicious with toasted sunflower or pumpkin seeds sprinkled on top.

Watercress Rice – Green Onion Rice – Parsley Rice

Serves 4-6

2 cups brown rice
½ cup watercress, green onion tops or
    parsley, sliced fine

Prepare rice according to preceding *Basic Short Grain Brown Rice* recipe. When serving, alternate layers of fresh green (watercress, green onion tops, or parsley) with hot rice in serving bowl, reserving the final bit to sprinkle on top. Green will soften and will be slightly cooked, while retaining its bright green color and fresh flavor.

Rice Balls

Makes 3

Rice balls are an ideal travel food. They might be called the original sandwich, having been enjoyed for centuries by Japanese away from home. The pickled plum in the center and the nori seaweed wrapped around the outside preserve the rice for several days—longer in winter, shorter in summer. Pressure cooked short grain brown rice holds together best. A small amount of sweet brown rice is a nice addition.

2 cups pressure cooked short grain
    brown rice
1-2 pickled plums *(umeboshi)*, depending on
    size, pits removed
2 sheets nori seaweed

With moistened hands, form firm balls of cooked brown rice. Keep a bowl of water nearby. Poke a hole in the center and insert a piece of plum. Reseal the hole.

Toast nori sea vegetable on both sides by waving gently over a hot burner (either gas or electric stoves work) until nori turns green. If toasting two sheets at a time, place smoother shiny sides together so rougher sides face heat source.

Fold and tear, or cut, nori in several pieces and cover rice ball by pressing seaweed around it with slightly moistened hands. For rice balls which will be eaten within two days, it isn't necessary to cover every bit of rice, but for any longer, be sure to cover thoroughly to avoid drying out.

Assorted Rice and Vegetable Rolls (Sushi)

Makes 2-3 sushi rolls

Sushi is the Japanese name for vinegared rice which is filled or topped with an array of flavorful vegetable (and/or fish) combinations, and often wrapped in nori seaweed. (The sushi sold in Japanese restaurants usually contains sugar and MSG.) As with rice balls, sushi are convenient travel foods. The pickled plum *(umeboshi)*, assorted pickles, and plum or rice vinegar on the inside combined with the sea vegetable on the outside act as natural preservatives to keep the grain fresh. Pressure cooked short grain brown rice holds together best. Sushi make delightful hors d'oeuvres as well.

These sushi rolls are called *nori-maki* or *maki-sushi*. Japanese horseradish (*wasabi*, see page 70) is a favorite, zesty addition to sushi, although it is not included in this recipe.

When serving large groups, it's easiest to do away with individual dip sauce bowls and to instead sprinkle the rice with flavorful, mildly salty, pickled plum *(ume)* vinegar instead of brown rice vinegar.

2 cups cooked short grain brown rice,
    firmly packed
2-3 sheets nori seaweed

1. LAY NORI HORIZONTALLY ON SQUARE SUSHI MAT.

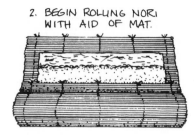

2. BEGIN ROLLING NORI WITH AID OF MAT.

3. CAREFULLY SLICE INTO DESIRED THICKNESS.

Filling No. 1:
  1 teaspoon rice vinegar (optional)
  2-5 pickled plums *(umeboshi)* depending on
      size, pits removed
  ¾ cup alfalfa sprouts (approximate)

Filling No. 2:
  1 teaspoon pickled plum *(ume)* vinegar
  3-6 long, thin strips carrot (or for brilliant
      color, 3 carrot strips and 6 red bell
      pepper strips, in season)
  2-3 green onions, tops only
      Pickled daikon radish *(takuan),* cut in
      thin strips

Dipping Sauce (optional):
  2 tablespoons good quality soy sauce
  2 tablespoons water

Cook carrot in water to cover until done, about five minutes. Add pepper strips, if used, in last two minutes and add green onion tops in last minute of cooking or leave raw-crisp. Drain and cool.

To prepare dipping sauce, simply mix ingredients and pour one to two tablespoons in individual serving cups.

To assemble sushi, have ready a small bowl filled with water to be used for moistening your hands and the far end of the sheet of nori. Sprinkle cooled rice with rice vinegar or pickled plum *(ume)* vinegar and toss gently to mix well. If nori has not been toasted, lightly toast sheets by slowly waving them over a flame (or electric stove burner) until color changes from purple to green. Packaged sheets which are folded as opposed to flat indicate nori has not been toasted.

Lay nori sheet horizontally on bamboo sushi mat or towel, shiny side down. Moisten hands, then take a handful of rice and place it on nori sheet. Press with fingers to spread rice over nori, just one or two kernels thick (or more for fatter sushi), to edges on three sides and to within one inch of the far edge.

For Filling No. 1, tear plums in small pieces and place in a line across rice one inch from the end nearest you. Spread sprouts on top of plums.

For Filling No. 2, lay two strips carrot, one green onion top, and several thin strips pickled daikon over rice one inch from the end nearest you.

Moisten the top end of nori for sealing roll after it's assembled. Roll up fairly tightly from end nearest you, pressing with sushi mat or towel while rolling, but try not to touch the rice with your fingers or the mat. Press to seal nori. With a sharp knife, cut sushi into thick or thin rounds. Wipe knife clean with a damp sponge or cloth for ease in cutting. Serve with ends up. Or, for travelling, leave sushi rolls whole.

Filling variations: Cucumber strips and toasted sesame seeds; carrot, green onion, wasabi, and marinated shiitake mushrooms; fermented soybeans *(natto)* with green *shiso* leaf or cucumber; *ume,* green *shiso* leaf, and cucumber; nut butter mixed with *ume,* miso, or soy sauce, with cooked *shiitake* mushroom and sprouts or green onion top; mashed tofu, miso, grated carrot, and green onion; dill pickle, mustard, and alfalfa sprouts; sauerkraut, sprouts, and mustard; *natto* miso and sprouts or cucumber; almost any leftovers.

Shaped Azuki Rice

*Makes 20 hand shapes
or 12 wooden mold shapes*

1 ¾ cups short grain brown rice
¼ cup azuki beans

Azuki rice is delicious served as is with a table seasoning, but when time allows, it's fun to use brown rice's sticky texture to form various shapes. Prepare according to *Basic Short Grain Brown Rice* recipe (see page 28), using pressure cooking technique, but boil beans vigorously in water to cover for 15 minutes before adding rinsed rice and enough extra water to equal three cups. Pressure cook for one hour with flame spreader under pot and over medium-low flame.

To cool rice quickly, spread it out on a baking sheet. Keep a bowl of water nearby and shape cooled rice into small, compact, round or oval shapes with moistened hands. Or purchase a Japanese wooden mold for pressing rice, available at Japanese kitchen shops. Mine has three different shapes and is easy to use. It's quicker than shaping by hand and nice for variety. Moisten the mold by immersing in water to keep the rice from sticking badly. Cookie cutters are another easy alternative.

One cup of cooked, firmly packed azuki rice makes five hand shapes or three wooden mold shapes. Figure two hand shapes or one mold shape per serving as part of the Japanese menu if rice rolls *(sushi)* are also being served. Leftover rice can be reheated to serve in a bowl at the side.

For added flavor and visual effect, sprinkle one fourth teaspoon table seasoning over each shape. Choose from homemade sesame salt or toasted sesame seeds (brown or black varieties) mixed with minced parsley; packaged sesame-miso-nori sprinkles; sesame-shiso-nori sprinkles; or shiso powder. You might also roll or dip just part of the shape in the seasoning. Arrange shapes on a pretty plate or on leaves.

Long Grain Brown Rice

Boiled long grain brown rice resembles white rice and has a similar light, fluffy texture. For these reasons, newcomers sometimes feel more comfortable starting with long grain brown rice. They gradually introduce short grain brown rice into their meals, at first boiled, and then pressure cooked. Often, when I am planning an international menu or a fancy meal for novices in the world of whole grain cuisine, I choose long grain brown rice because of this greater familiarity.

For large amounts, figure one cup dry long grain brown rice serves three to four. Use the finger method to determine water quantity, measuring water two inches above rice.

Here are two methods for preparing long grain brown rice:

Basic Long Grain Brown Rice Recipe No. 1

Serves about 6
Makes 5 cups

2 cups long grain brown rice
3 cups water
¼ teaspoon sea salt

Rinse rice. Place ingredients in saucepan of appropriate size and bring to boil. Turn flame low to simmer, covered, for one hour. Place flame spreader under pot after one half hour.

Basic Long Grain Brown Rice Recipe No. 2

Serves about 6
Makes about 5½ cups

2 cups long grain brown rice
4 cups water
¼ teaspoon sea salt

For the fluffiest long grain rice, rinse, then roast rice in an unoiled skillet until it is dry and mildly fragrant. Bring water and salt to boil, add rice, and when boiling resumes, place flame spreader under pot to cook over medium-low heat for one hour.

Mexican Rice (Sopa Seca de Arroz)

Serves 5-8

Two kinds of soups are served in Mexico. One is the broth called *caldo*, served at the beginning of the meal. The other is the dry soup — which is actually a main grain dish, as are tortillas. Dry soups are usually made of rice or noodles cooked in a stock. *Sopa seca de arroz* translates to mean dry rice soup. The stock is entirely absorbed in cooking. Both kinds are served only on special occasions, the dry soup being served right after the liquid one. I find it easier to add the vegetables and sauce after, instead of before, the rice is cooked. The colors are much brighter and fresher this way.

Rice:
2 cups long grain brown rice
4 cups water
6 inch piece kombu sea vegetable
1 tablespoon good quality soy sauce

Vegetables:
1 tablespoon corn oil (optional)
½ cup onion, minced
¼ cup peas, shelled
¼ cup carrot, diced small
2 cloves garlic, minced
½ cup *Mexican Red Sauce*
¼ cup parsley, minced

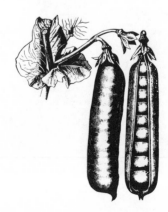

Mexican Red Sauce:

Makes 3 cups

1 pound carrots (or winter squash or
    pumpkin), about 4 cups
1 medium beet
1 cup water
1 bay leaf
1 teaspoon oregano
2 tablespoons good quality soy sauce

To prepare stock for cooking rice, bring water, kombu, and soy sauce to boil and slow boil five minutes. Remove kombu and add rinsed rice. Return to boil, cover, place flame spreader under pot, and cook covered over medium-low flame for one hour.

Vegetables may be steamed or sautéed. To steam, cook onion, peas, and carrot 10-15 minutes, adding garlic in last five minutes. To sauté, heat oil and sauté onion briefly, then add other vegetables and cook until soft.

To prepare sauce, cut vegetables in one-inch chunks, then place all ingredients except oregano and soy sauce in pressure cooker and pressure cook five minutes. Remove bay leaf. While ingredients are still hot, puree in blender with oregano and soy sauce until creamy smooth. Reserve extra sauce to serve over noodles, or in any way you would use tomato sauce.

To assemble, add red sauce and parsley to vegetables and mix well, then add cooked rice and mix in, taking care not to mash rice. Heat to serve.

For large amounts, such as 60 people, figure that this recipe serves 8.

Wheat

Wheat shares the number one spot with rice for the food eaten by more people on the planet than any other. The wheats are the most important cereals in temperate climates, providing the staple food—bread. Wheat is the native grain for most present-day Americans of European heritage.

Bread wheat is grown in Europe, the Soviet Union, Asia, Australia, Canada, and the Americas. Hard wheat grains are rich in protein which occurs in the stretchy, gluten portion, and this allows bread to rise. Soft wheat is lighter in color, softer in texture, richer in starch, and lower in gluten, and thus used for pastries that don't need to rise. The flour from another variety, durum wheat, is actually second in importance to bread wheat; it is the best kind for making pasta because of its high proportion of gluten.

Wheat is rarely served in the whole form because it takes so long to become soft and digestible, even with a pressure cooker. Do try the *Brown Rice with Wheat Berries* recipe (see page 28), a simple grain dish in which wheat berries add color and texture.

Usually wheat is ground in varying degrees of fineness to make a wide range of favorite foods including breakfast cereals, pilaf, breads, muffins, crackers, noodles, and wheatmeat. Freshly-ground wheat flour is flour the way it's meant to be—but until you can arrange this experience for yourself, enjoy store-bought, organic whole wheat bread and pastry flours. Store flour in a cool, dry, dark place or the refrigerator to prevent rancidity.

Wheat Pilaf

Serves 3-4

Wheat pilaf is bulgur, vegetables, and noodles cooked in a hot, seasoned stock. It serves as a main dish or stuffing, or as an ingredient in loaves or burgers. Pilaf is easy to make and much higher in quality than the store-bought mixes which also contain beef fat, sugar, potato starch, beef extract, and caramel coloring. Soy sauce replaces the rich flavor and color of beef in this version.

Bulgur is whole wheat which has been parboiled, dried, and cracked. The boiling process transfers nutrients from the bran into the grain; then the depleted bran is partially removed and the grain is cracked. Bulgur retains most of the bran and the germ.

    1 teaspoon corn oil
    1 cup onions
    ½ cup mushrooms
    ½ cup celery (1 stalk)
    2 cloves garlic, minced
    1 cup bulgur wheat
    ½ cup whole wheat ribbon noodles or
        vegetable macaroni
    3 cups water
    1 tablespoon good quality soy sauce
    ½ teaspoon oregano
    2 tablespoons parsley, minced, for garnish

Dice vegetables small. Heat oil and sauté vegetables briefly, then add bulgur and noodles and stir well. Meanwhile, in a separate pot, bring water, soy sauce, and oregano to boil. Add to vegetables and return to boil, then turn flame low to simmer, covered, for one-half hour. Gently fluff bulgur with fork to serve, garnished.

For large amounts, such as for 60 people, simply multiply ingredients by 20 except water which should reach three inches above bulgur, about 40 cups.

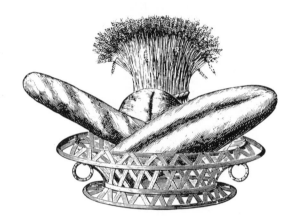

Breads

Whole grain bread is the staple food for many of the world's people. Most varieties are based on wheat because of its high gluten content which gives dough its elasticity, and, with time, the ability to rise. When cooked grains, such as rice or fermented grains such as a sourdough starter, are added to whole wheat flour, leavening time is cut in half. Water hastens fermentation as well, so a batter bread cultures more quickly than a drier bread.

Nowadays most bakers use shortcuts such as commercial yeast, baking powder, and baking soda to leaven their breads. But bread dough will rise naturally of its own accord without the introduction of a commercial leavening agent. Within 12-36 hours (or half the time when sourdough is added), depending on the temperature and humidity, wild yeasts in the air feed on the carbohydrates in the dough, converting them into more digestible forms and into carbon dioxide which forms air pockets. You can watch this fascinating process take place every time you make bread by the natural rise method.

Jacques de Langre of the Grain and Salt Society (P.O. Box DD, Magalia, CA 95945) has introduced these methods to most people who practice it in the U.S. He has met with many bakers in France and Belgium where there is more widely available information on the negative effects of ingesting yeasted and unnaturally leavened bread on a daily basis: stomach lining irritated, intestinal flora killed, enzymes in the bread destroyed, and the possible causation of rickets, nervous disorders, and cancer. Of course, it's alright to eat yeasted bread once in a while, but for daily consumption, home-baked, naturally-risen bread made with organically grown, freshly ground wheat is best.

The following three recipes are the versions I have developed after studying with Jacques and other bakers, and then practicing and teaching on my own. The thing I do differently is to add warm, salted water to the flour. I feel this process thoroughly dissolves the salt and softens the hard particles of flour—especially fresh-ground flour—making the dough easier to work with.

Natural Rise Whole Wheat Bread

Makes 1 large loaf or 2 small loaves

The most important part of the breadmaking process is the attention you give it. After just a few times, when you actually have seen the dough change, knowing when to put it in the oven will come naturally. When you look at and feel the dough at intervals during rising, you will see, feel, and smell slight changes taking place. Nothing may happen for hours, but then the dough will become light and airy and will spread out in the bowl. The smell will be sweet, perhaps very slightly sour. This is when the dough is ready to be baked. If your bread comes out "like a brick" or tastes quite sour, you haven't tuned in to this natural leavening process.

6 cups whole wheat flour
2½ cups water
¾ teaspoon sea salt

Heat, but don't boil, water and salt. Add to flour, mix well and knead to form a very smooth dough, about 100 times. Moisten hands several times if dough sticks with kneading. Place dough in bowl, cover with two damp, natural fiber cloths (soak cloths, then wring them out), and set in a warm place.

Check at least every eight hours to be sure towels are not dried out and that the loaf is still moist. If it isn't, don't give up hope. If the top is just slightly dry, knead it and re-cover; but if the top is very dried out and a hard crust has formed, scrape it off and discard it or soak that part in water until it softens and knead it back in.

When texture lightens up, gently form loaf (loaves) and place in corn-oiled bread pan(s) or pie pan(s) for round loaves. Cover again with just one damp cloth and return dough to a warm place to proof (rise) for one to two hours before baking. If the dough has lightened up again and is so relaxed it has spread out somewhat in the pan after only one hour, it's ready to bake. Remove towel and slit top halfway through or press a wet cookie cutter shape into surface of round dough for a whimsical effect. Place pan(s) in a cold oven, then set temperature to 400 degrees and bake for one-half to one hour. This saves on fuel and allows the bread to rise gradually as the heat increases. Or preheat oven to 400 degrees, then bake bread. Either way, check after one-half hour to see if bread looks done—is firm with no wet spots and has a golden brown color on all sides.

Brown Rice Bread

Makes 1 large loaf or 2 small loaves

3 cups whole wheat flour
3 cups cooked brown rice, well packed
1½ cups water
½ teaspoon sea salt

Mix flour and rice well by rubbing with hands between palms. Proceed as for preceding *Natural Rise Whole Wheat Bread,* starting with less water as the amount needed depends on the moistness of the rice. This bread often takes half the rising time of plain whole wheat bread.

6 cups whole wheat flour
1-2 cups water
1 cup sourdough starter
¾ teaspoon sea salt

Sourdough Starter:
2 cups whole wheat flour
2 cups water
(No salt)

To make sourdough starter, mix flour and water in a large jar to prevent foaming over. Leave at room temperature for 2-6 days, stirring one to two times daily. Bubbles and a mildly sour smell develop as mixture ferments. Store in a cool place and use at least once a week.

To make sourdough bread, mix water with starter and salt, then add to flour to form dough. Amount of water depends on texture of sourdough starter; for example, if starter is already watery, use smaller amount of liquid. Proceed as for *Natural Rise Whole Wheat Bread* on preceding page. Rising time is cut in half.

To replenish starter, add a small hunk of dough or more flour and water to starter on a regular basis (once a day is best). If water becomes very grey and very sour, start again.

Whole Wheat Sourdough Bread

Makes 1 large loaf or 2 small loaves

Sourdough is just that . . . sour dough. There is no mystery to preparing sourdough starter although you might think so from the packaged products available in supermarkets. Some brands even contain sugar and yeast. Real, homemade sourdough ferments naturally and, when used to make bread, causes the whole dough to ferment and rise quickly. In a warm room, the dough in this recipe is ready in only seven hours.

Quick Breads

Quick breads may be shaped and baked right away. Because of their smaller size, they bake thoroughly even though they haven't risen. However, a rising time of several hours to overnight or even a full natural rise gives the breads a softer, lighter texture. Either way, they're great and always appreciated.

Sesame Breadsticks

*Makes eight 6-inch sticks
or four 12-inch sticks*

1 cup whole wheat flour
⅓ cup water
1 tablespoon corn oil
⅛ teaspoon sea salt
2 tablespoons sesame seeds, toasted

In saucepan, heat but do not boil water, oil, and salt. Add to flour, mix well, then form a smooth dough. Let sit covered with a damp cloth in a warm area until ready to bake—the longer the better for a lighter texture—or heat oven to 350 degrees to bake immediately.

Sprinkle seeds on board and knead into dough when ready to bake, or divide dough into four or eight equal portions and roll out onto seeds. Bake on corn-oiled sheet for 20 minutes for soft bread sticks, or one-half hour for firmer sticks, turning once halfway through.

For large amounts, figure one-and-one-half sticks per person, as some people won't take two.

Variation: Use half the amount of black sesame seeds, available at Oriental food stores.

Wild Nori Crackers

Makes 1 dozen 2″ × 3″ crackers

Sea vegetable foraging is one of our greatest joys here on the north coast of California where wild nori grows abundantly.

Follow *Sesame Breadsticks* recipe above to prepare dough, but substitute one tablespoon toasted wild nori flakes (or the packaged cultivated nori flakes or dulse sea vegetable) for sesame seeds. Mix nori with flour before adding heated ingredients.

To make wild nori flakes, simply spread dried wild nori on a baking sheet and bake at 350 degrees until color changes to green, about five minutes. Overcooking causes a bitter flavor.

To make crackers, roll dough out, then place on a corn-oiled baking sheet and roll out even thinner, about one-eighth inch. Cut into squares or diamond shapes or use a pastry wheel, or cookie cutter. Bake at 350 degrees for 15-20 minutes.

Journeycakes

Serves 12

This flat bread represents the exchange between the Native Americans and the early settlers. Corn and wheat come together in "journeycakes," a favorite bread of Thoreau. (I've added the seeds and oil.) An ideal travel food, we always include journeycakes in picnic and travel menus.

3 cups corn flour or cornmeal
3 cups whole wheat flour
2 cups water
2-6 tablespoons corn oil (optional)
¾ teaspoon sea salt
½ cup pumpkin and/or sunflower seeds, toasted

Mix flours well. Heat together but don't boil water, oil, and salt and add to flours to form a moist dough. Knead 100 times and cover with a damp cloth to rise overnight in a warm place.

For one large loaf, leave dough whole, or separate into two to four equal portions, either way forming round, flat loaves which are one inch thick. Sprinkle seeds on top and press them in place with rolling pin. Bake on corn-oiled sheet for one-half hour at 350 degrees, turning loaves over after 20 minutes.

Blue and Yellow Cornmeal Muffins or Corn Sticks

Makes 1 dozen medium-sized muffins, or 1 dozen small muffins and 7 sticks

Blue whole-grain corn such as Hopi blue corn and cornmeal comes from the southwestern Indians and is becoming more widely available in high quality natural food stores. Use it just as you would yellow cornmeal. For a special treat, make two batches of this recipe, one from yellow and one from blue cornmeal.

Tofu is used as a leavener here (two ounces soft tofu per cup of flour) instead of the usual eggs and/or baking powder.

My favorite pans for these muffins are made of cast iron with small scalloped cups, or corn stick pans which must be very well oiled for easy removal.

Great with *Sunflower Sage Spread* (see page 81)!

2 cups corn flour or meal (yellow or blue)
1 cup whole wheat pastry flour
6 ounces tofu, soft and fresh
3 cups water
½ teaspoon sea salt

For a wonderful crust, heat oven to 400 degrees. Place well corn-oiled muffin tins or corn stick pans in oven to heat while you are mixing ingredients.

To prepare batter, mix flours well. Crumble tofu into blender. Bring water and salt to boil and add immediately to tofu to blend very briefly, less than creamy smooth. Immediately add to flour and mix well. Spoon into hot muffin tins and bake for one-half hour. Let cool somewhat before serving for best texture.

Whole Grain Noodles

Whole grain noodles are a quick and easy alternative or side dish for cooked whole grains such as rice. One of the most popular foods in the world, they are easy to cook, fun to eat, and adapt to every kind of meal from the simplest to the most elaborate. Since noodles are cooked in water, they are soft and easy to digest. Today noodles are made from wheat, rice, buckwheat, corn, and even soybeans or jerusalem artichokes. Add noodles to soup or make them the central focus in casseroles and salads as in these recipes.

Nutty Noodle Bake

Serves 6
Makes about 2 cups

This simple, dairyless dish has an eggy texture and a cheeselike topping.

2 cups cooked *jinenjo soba* or other noodles
½ cup almonds, toasted and chopped

Creamy Herb Sauce:
1 pound tofu, soft and fresh
¼ cup fresh cilantro or basil, or 2 heaping
     teaspoons dry herbs
½ teaspoon sea salt

Topping:
¼ cup sesame tahini
¼ cup water
1 tablespoon good quality soy sauce

To make sauce, place ingredients in blender and puree until creamy smooth. Add water only if necessary to blend.

Mix sauce with cooked noodles and nuts and pour into a small (one-and-one-half quart), lightly-oiled casserole dish.

Mix topping ingredients and drizzle over top so entire surface is covered. Bake in 350 degree oven for one-half hour.

This recipe works well for large amounts with ingredients simply increased by multiplying.

Pasta Patricio

Serves 3 as main dish, 4-6 as side dish

For my husband Patrick, my version of "Fettucine Alfredo" without the butter, cheese, cream, and egg. Whole wheat udon noodles are shaped just like fettucine noodles, so they work

well here. If they aren't available, substitute whole wheat ribbons, spaghetti, or spiral noodles.

Italian White Sauce really satisfies the desire for dairy foods, especially cheese, and for rich Italian flavors.

  ½ pound dry whole wheat noodles
  2 cups *Italian White Sauce*
  2 tablespoons parsley, minced for garnish

Italian White Sauce:

Makes about 4 cups

  1 tablespoon olive oil
  2 large onions, sliced thin
  4 large cloves garlic, minced
  1 pound tofu, soft and fresh
  ¼ cup good quality soy sauce
  1 heaping teaspoon each oregano and basil
  Up to ½ cup water (optional)

To prepare sauce, sauté onions in oil until soft. Add garlic and herbs, crumble tofu into pan, and drizzle soy sauce over all. Cover to cook over medium-low heat about 10 minutes.

Blend until creamy smooth or blend just half the mixture for a more chunky effect. Add water only if a lighter texture is desired or to make blending easier.

Cook and drain noodles and place in serving bowl. Add sauce and mix well. Serve garnished with parsley. It goes fast!

This recipe works well for large amounts with ingredients simply increased by multiplying.

Wheatmeat

Wheatmeat is a wheat-based food which looks, feels, and even tastes like meat. Everyone enjoys its satisfying, rich flavor and juicy, substantial texture.

Known as "seitan" (pronounced say-tahn) in Japan and "gluten" in the west, wheatmeat was first introduced to Japan from China by Buddhist monks. The monks found that a vegetarian diet, centered around grains and vegetables, was conducive to spiritual development because it allowed the body to function in a peaceful manner. Wheatmeat is also known to give strength and vitality.

Delicious and easy to digest, wheatmeat is a high-protein food. Made from wheat gluten, the part of the wheat kernel containing protein, wheatmeat is cooked in a soy broth, making for even greater protein value. Wheatmeat enriches any dish in which it is prepared.

Since it takes time to prepare wheatmeat (about 20 to 30 minutes of actual hands-on time mixing, kneading, and hand-washing, and about one-half hour for soaking and cooking), it becomes a special food reserved for festive occasions or whenever you want to make people extra happy.

After 10 years of making wheatmeat by various methods and with varying degrees of success, I attended a class with Cornellia Aihara at the VEGA Macrobiotic Center (1511 Robinson, Oroville, CA 95965). In minutes we learned this simple method which is almost foolproof, especially if you are in a class watching it being done.

Wheatmeat Recipe

Makes 2-3 cups cooked or 12-16 ounces

Wheatmeat Dough:
    4 cups whole wheat flour (use finely ground
        hard red spring wheat which is highest
        in gluten)
2-2½ cups warm water

Wheatmeat Cooking Broth:
    2 cups water
¼-½ cup good quality soy sauce
    6 inch piece kombu sea vegetable

To make wheatmeat dough, place flour in large bowl and add water. Mix to form a wet, smooth dough. With dough still in the bowl, knead with moistened hands (to avoid sticking) or just mix 50 times to develop the elasticity of the gluten.

Cover dough with lukewarm water for 15 minutes, then pour water off and replace with cold water. Wash the dough in the same large

bowl, placed in the kitchen sink in case of spillage. Gently at first, then more vigorously, knead and stretch dough under water so the white starch and the brown bran flakes come out into the water, leaving the stretchy, protein-rich gluten. Feel for any gritty parts where bran is still incorporated in the mass. How smooth you make your wheatmeat is up to you. The water will need to be changed until it stays almost clear after kneading, about three times. The process takes 10-20 minutes—less, after you've done it a few times. Pour off the washing liquid and save the bran and starch parts that settle on the bottom for use in thickening stews, puddings, or gravies.

To prepare wheatmeat cooking broth, bring ingredients to rolling boil in a saucepan. Tear off walnut-size pieces of wheatmeat dough or simply cut dough in chunks or slices. Add to boiling stock, then keep broth at moderate boil to cook for 15 minutes. Wheatmeat will double in size.

Broth variations: To flavor broth, add one or more of the following seasonings—1 bay leaf; 2 cloves garlic, minced; 1 teaspoon ginger, fresh grated.

Corn

Corn is the only cereal crop of American origin. (Wild rice is actually a grass which is native to North America.) Brought to Europe by Columbus, it has since spread to all parts of the world. The U.S. is the world's largest producer, but most of America's native grain is now used for feeding livestock, especially pigs. As food for humans, corn is most important as the staple food in South America where it is eaten as tortillas, and in South and East Africa where it is made into a cereal gruel. In Italy, cornmeal is made into polenta. North American corn dishes include corn bread, corn pone, hominy, Indian pudding, sweet corn-on-the-cob, and popcorn.

Since corn is the native grain of the Americas, it seems fitting that we should learn how to prepare and enjoy it. Because it is such a hard grain when dried, it is usually ground into meal or flour for cooking. However, Native Americans knew how to make the whole grain soft and digestible. They found that by adding wood ashes to the cooking grain, the hard outer layer cracked and fell off or was easily removed by rubbing, leaving the tender kernels called *hominy* intact. Hominy was served as is or in combination with beans or vegetables in stews. Often it was mashed to form a whole corn dough called *masa*. Masa was then shaped into many traditional forms such as tortillas, *arepas*, and dumplings. The liquid left from cooking hominy makes a delicious beverage.

Traditional Whole Corn (Hominy), Hominy Tea, and Whole Corn Dough (Masa)

Makes about 6 cups hominy and 2 cups hominy tea

Wood ashes should be made from clean hardwood, free of paint and preservatives, and from a fire started with natural materials such as leaves or dry brush instead of newspaper which contains chemicals. Ash from different kinds of wood varies in degree of alkalinity, and so its effectiveness will vary in softening the hull. When ashes cool, sift to store in covered container. To use in cooking, loosely tie up measured amount of ashes in two thicknesses of cheesecloth.

2 cups whole dry corn
8 cups water (4 cups for soaking and first cooking with ashes, 4 cups for second cooking)
½ cup sifted wood ashes

Soak corn overnight in a stainless steel pressure cooker with four cups water. (Stainless steel cookware is preferred over aluminum in macrobiotic cooking, especially in this case. The lye in the wood ash reacts strongly with aluminum to produce hydrogen gas, which is both flammable and explosive.)

In the morning, add bag of ashes. Squeeze bag to permeate water with ashes. Bring to pressure and cook for one hour. Check corn at this time to see if hulls have loosened and corn is soft. If not, return to pressure to cook one-half hour more, or add more ashes and water to cook longer.

If corn has softened, remove bag, drain liquid (good for the garden), and carefully rinse the corn until the water is completely clear. Rub the corn between your palms to loosen the hulls while rinsing. Return corn to pressure with four cups fresh water and cook one-half to one hour more (less if corn is soft, more if still rather hard).

Strain out and reserve hominy broth from the final cooking to serve as a tea or in soups. Use hominy as is (see *Pinto Beans and Hominy* recipe, page 76) or grind cooked corn in a steel mill to make whole corn dough *(masa)*. Knead dough very briefly, just to form a cohesive ball.

Cracked Corn, Cornmeal, and Corn Flour

A wide variety of foods made from ground corn have been enjoyed historically by people throughout the world. Nowadays most ground corn recipes also call for dairy products, eggs, sugar, excessive quantities of salt and oil, and commercial leavening agents such as baking powder, baking soda, and yeast. In many cases, these undesirable foods were not used in the original versions. Using macrobiotic sense, we can upgrade the quality of present-day corn recipes and enjoy even more delicious results. Of course, fresh-ground corn is the very best for flavor and nutrition. One cup whole corn yields about one-and-one-half cups meal or flour.

Polenta Squares with Red Vegetable Sauce

Serves 16

Much of the polenta available commercially is ground corn which has first had the germ removed in order to extract the oil. Both coarsely ground cornmeal and corn flour have had the germ ground up with the rest of the kernel, making them more complete foods.

Polenta is made like cornmeal mush, with the difference that it is cooked until a spoon stands up in the mush, about one hour.

Polenta:

2 cups cornmeal or flour
6 cups water
1 tablespoon good quality soy sauce or
　½ teaspoon sea salt

Italian Red Sauce:

Makes 2½ cups

1 pound carrots (or winter squash or
　pumpkin), about 4 cups
1 medium beet
½ cup water
1 bay leaf
1 teaspoon each oregano and basil
2 tablespoons good quality soy sauce,
　sauerkraut juice, or miso

Red Vegetable Sauce:

¼ cup water
1 onion, cut in thin slices
3 cups broccoli, cut in 2 inch lengths, then
　in ¼ inch strips lengthwise, keeping
　flowerettes intact
1½ cup *Italian Red Sauce*

To make polenta, bring ingredients to boil, then simmer, uncovered, for one hour. Stir about every 10 minutes. Pour hot cornmeal mush into standard eight-inch square baking dish to set, about one hour at room temperature.

Italian Red Sauce resembles tomato sauce in texture, appearance, and flavor. Notice that it is the same as the *Mexican Red Sauce* recipe with the addition of basil which is used in Italian but not in Mexican cuisine. A little less water is used here as well.

Place vegetables in pressure cooker with water and bay leaf. Bring to pressure, then turn flame to medium-low and time for five minutes.

Discard bay leaf and puree ingredients with seasonings and soy sauce in blender. Use miso only if you are not serving it in another dish at the meal.

To prepare vegetables, place water, onion, and broccoli in saucepan and bring to boil. Simmer covered until done, about 10 minutes.

Heat *Italian Red Sauce*.

To assemble dish, cut gelled polenta into 16 squares. Top each square with a little onion and broccoli and a dollop of the sauce.

For large volumes of this recipe, simply multiply ingredients.

Millet

Millet has been cultivated since prehistoric times in southern Europe and Asia. It was a sacred plant in China as early as 2700 B.C. and was also known to the Lake Dwellers in Europe. It was the "milium" of the Romans, and reference is made to its use for making bread in the Old Testament. Millet is nutritious, containing carbohydrates plus ten percent protein and four percent fat. Its chief agricultural virtues are its capacity to produce a moderate yield even on very poor soil and to withstand both drought and waterlogging better than most crops.

For most people, millet is usually the third grain in popularity after brown rice and whole wheat bread. Millet cooks in half the time of brown rice, has a pleasing flavor of its own, and a lovely yellow color. It has a drier, flakier texture than rice and, for this reason, is a nice base for vegetable stews. Millet also makes an excellent pie crust, especially nice for people who don't want to eat flour products (see *Sunshine Pie* recipe, page 58).

Vegetable Millet

Serves 3-4
Makes 4 cups

1 teaspoon sesame oil
½ medium onion, cut in ½ inch cubes
1 cup butternut or buttercup squash, cut in
    ½ inch cubes
¼ cup burdock (if available), sliced
    lengthwise, then across in ¼ inch slices,
    or ½ cup celery, cut in ½ inch cubes
1 cup millet
2½ cups water
¼ teaspoon sea salt

Heat oil and sauté onion briefly over medium-low heat, or omit oil and simply dry roast millet in cooking pot. Add squash and burdock or celery and stir, then add rinsed millet and stir until it dries out somewhat and releases a nutty aroma. Add water and salt and bring to boil

over high heat. Cover, turn flame to low, and simmer one-half hour. Gently spoon millet and vegetables into serving bowl to fluff the millet without mashing the squash.

For large amounts, just multiply ingredient quantities except water, which is only two cups per one cup millet.

Variation: Millet sets quickly when allowed to cool and so is ideal for making a quick, simple loaf or pie. Simply pat hot millet in lightly-oiled loaf or pie pan.

Oats

Oats existed in Europe during the Bronze Age (3000-2000 BC).

Oats are used for human food whole, cut or cracked, rolled into flakes, or ground into flour. Whole oats have a wonderful, full flavor not found in cracked or rolled oats. Steel-cut oats are whole oat groats that are sliced with steel knives into thirds, quarters, and halves to shorten cooking time for the rich, chunky traditional porridge known as Scotch Oats. (See *Irish Oatmeal with Dulse* recipe, page 18). The best rolled oats are made from organically grown oat groats which are rolled without the destructive high-heat steaming and kiln-drying process used with the commercial type. Since oat flour has antioxidant properties, it is often mixed commercially with other flours to help delay deterioration.

Rye

Rye is an important crop in the colder parts of northern and central Europe and Russia, where it is grown as far north as the Arctic Circle and in mountainous areas 14,000 feet above sea level. It is a relative newcomer to cultivation, found in Iron Age sites in Europe. Rye can be grown on poor soils where other cereals would not be productive. It is similar to wheat in composition and its use as a food source is chiefly in making black bread and Scandinavian rye crisp bread. (See *Rice with Wild Rice and Rye Berries* recipe, page 28, for one way to use whole rye.)

Barley

Barley was the dominant cereal in Europe in the Neolithic and Bronze Ages (8000-5000 B.C. and 3000-2000 B.C. respectively) and was used by the Greeks and Romans around 500 B.C.

The barley used today in soups and stews is *pearled* which means the husk and bran layers have been removed to varying degrees. Whole grain barley is rarely available. Another type used in macrobiotic cooking comes from the Orient and is called pearl barley, Job's tears, wild barley, or *hato mugi* in Japanese. Whole grain pearl barley adds a deep flavor to the dishes in which it is cooked. (See *Pearl Barley Rice* recipe, page 28.)

Buckwheat

Buckwheat originated in Siberia and Manchuria, and spread throughout Asia, the Middle East, and Europe. German and Dutch settlers brought it to the U.S. In Russia and Eastern Europe, buckwheat is still used as a staple grain food and in making bread, pudding, cake, and beer. In the U.S. in the 1860s, buckwheat was used ten times more than it is today.

Buckwheat's name was derived from a Dutch term, *bockweit*, meaning "beech wheat" because of the seeds' resemblance to beechnuts and nutritional qualities similar to wheat. Buckwheat is not a true grain, but is nutritionally on a par with the grains. Botanically it belongs to the Buckwheat family (Polygonaceae) which includes dock and rhubarb. Cereal grains belong to the Gramineae family. Buckwheat looks more like a bush than a slender stemmed reed.

Buckwheat adapts to poor soil and moist, cool climates; it is hardy and easily grown. For this reason, it is not usually doused with insecticides.

Buckwheat seeds are called "groats," and when toasted are called *kasha*. See the recipe for *Buckwheat Noodles (Soba) in Light Ginger-Soy Broth* on page 23.

Table Seasonings

Table seasonings, also called condiments, are foods which are used in small amounts to enhance the flavor of whole grains and noodles, and vegetable or bean dishes. Mildly salty in taste, they are sprinkled on at the table. Table seasonings are easy to carry on trips or to restaurants.

When serving packaged table seasonings to your family or guests for the first few times, place the package nearby so they can familiarize themselves with the description and ingredients. Because of their rich flavors, for large amounts figure about one teaspoon per serving, except for the *Sesame Shiso Sprinkles* which contain mostly seeds and might be estimated at one or two level tablespoons per serving.

Some Commercially Available Varieties

Sesame-Nori-Miso Sprinkles, called *goma-miso furikake* in Japanese, are a combination of dried barley miso, whole toasted sesame seeds, and green nori sea vegetable flakes.

Sesame Miso Powder, goma muso in Japanese, is a blend of 60 percent barley miso and 40 percent sesame butter which is lightly toasted to make a crumbly powder.

Sesame Shiso Sprinkles contain toasted whole sesame seeds, powdered pickled *shiso* leaves (see next condiment description), and green nori sea vegetable flakes. I usually add more dried *shiso* leaves to this combination for more flavor—about one-eighth teaspoon of shiso per tablespoon of condiment *or* one-and-a-half teaspoons per three-quarter cup package.

Shiso Powder, shiso momiji in Japanese, is made from the red herb leaves and stems of the perilla or beefsteak plant. They are pickled with the *umeboshi* plum for color and flavor, and then sun-dried and finely chopped. Rich in calcium and iron, their zesty flavor adds tang to any dish or dressing.

Vegetable Miso Seasoning, called *tekka*, is a hearty condiment. Root vegetables (carrot, burdock root, lotus root, and ginger root) are sautéed in sesame oil and cooked with plain soybean *(hatcho)* miso over a low fire for several hours until a crumbly powder is formed. The Japanese word *tekka* means iron fire because the seasoning is prepared in a cast iron pan and, partially for this reason, is known to be high in that mineral.

Note: One source for these seasonings and other macrobiotic quality foods from Japan is Granum Inc., 2901 N.E. Blakeley Street, Seattle, WA 98105.

Lightly Toasted Seeds and Nuts

Lightly toasted seeds and nuts taste better than raw ones. Flavor is greatly improved as the oil is brought to the surface with cooking.

Besides enhancing grain and vegetable dishes, nuts and seeds are tasty additions to salads, breads, snacks like trail mix, and desserts. Even though they are available in most natural food stores, toasting at home assures freshness, and allows you to determine the degree of toasting and the amount of soy sauce to add, if desired. And besides, it's easy and cheaper than store-bought varieties.

Have you ever read the label on a typical jar of dry roasted peanuts? It contains "peanuts, salt, modified food starch, gum arabic and/or dextrin, MSG, yeast, paprika, and other spices." For real flavor without the additives, try these recipes, and make enough to last a week or two.

Sesame Salt

Makes 20 or more servings or about 1¼ cups

Sesame salt is by far the favorite table seasoning used by macrobiotic and many other health-conscious people. Known as *gomashio* in Japanese, *goma* meaning sesame and *shio* salt, its delicious and healthful qualities seem to have made it the ideal topping for brown rice. Sesame salt is commercially available, but to be assured of overall freshness and high quality sea salt used in reasonable amounts, it's best to make your own on a weekly basis. Also, commercial sesame salt tends to be minimally pulverized with mostly whole seeds showing. Grind it more at home for greater flavor and assimilation.

Because of the salt content, sesame salt is known to help neutralize an acid blood condition. In this form, however, salt is combined with oil and does not stimulate the body as much as plain salt does. The ratio of seeds to salt in this recipe is 16:1 or 1 cup:1 tablespoon. This is a delicious, mild sesame salt. For those who wish to cut down further on their salt intake, figure 1 or 2 teaspoons sea salt per cup of seeds instead.

1 cup whole sesame seeds
1 tablespoon good quality sea salt

To prepare seeds, rinse by swishing in a bowl of cool water to cover. Light stems float to the top and any heavier particles, such as sand, sink to the bottom. Quickly pour off surface liquid and catch seeds in a strainer except last few where sand may remain. (Some batches of sesame seeds are completely clean and don't require this first step.)

Good quality sea salt is moist and must be briefly dried for easy grinding. Heat skillet and add salt. Stir until salt looks dry, about one to two minutes over medium heat. Transfer salt to serrated ceramic mortar (called a *suribachi* in Japanese) and grind briefly to pulverize.

Add rinsed seeds to skillet and stir over medium heat until seeds are dry and crush easily between the pressure of two fingers, about five minutes. If seeds pop a lot, heat is too high. Or spread seeds on a baking sheet and toast in a 350 degree oven, 10 to 15 minutes. Add seeds to salt in mortar and grind together until half the seeds are pulverized, about five to 10 minutes. Or use a blender, but briefly, or you may end up with seed "butter."

A comfortable position for grinding is seated with the mortar settled in your lap. Use the wooden pestle to grind by stirring in an orderly circular motion. The oil in the seeds coats the salt and both are pulverized, rendering them more digestible. Sesame seeds are so tiny that they often end up leaving the body whole if they are not thoroughly chewed or ground up.

Make enough sesame salt for a week and store it in a sealed glass or pottery jar. When we make this condiment in cooking classes, everyone takes their turn grinding. A smile alights on each face in turn as the rich toasted sesame aroma rises. A good activity for children or anyone with idle hands. Figure one level tablespoon per serving for large groups.

Toasted Sunflower or Pumpkin Seeds (or any nuts or seeds)

Makes 2 cups

2 cups sunflower or pumpkin seeds
1-2 tablespoons good quality soy sauce

Simply place seeds (or nuts) on a dry baking sheet and bake at 350 degrees or cook over a medium flame in a dry skillet, stirring often. When they begin to turn golden brown in color and you smell the tantalizing aroma, about 10-15 minutes, sprinkle seeds or nuts with soy sauce (or spray with a mister), then stir well so soy sauce is well distributed. Cook about one minute more to dry seeds. For large groups, figure one to two level tablespoons per serving.

Nori-Nut Trail/Party Mix

Makes 2½ cups

This recipe is an expanded version of G.O.R.P. (Good Old Raisins and Peanuts) with a delightful new taste.

½ cup each sunflower seeds, almonds, and peanuts, toasted and sprinkled with good quality soy sauce (see previous recipe)

½ cup raisins

2 sheets nori seaweed

Toast nori sheets by holding shiny sides together and gently waving sheets about two inches above a medium flame or heated electric burner until color changes from purple/black to green, about one minute. Or for large amounts, place nori sheets on a cookie sheet in a 350 degree oven until toasted, for about two minutes. Sushi nori is already toasted.

Cut toasted nori in half-inch squares and mix with other ingredients.

Vegetables from Land and Sea

Vegetables are the third most important group of plants which serve the human race as food, after cereals and legumes and root crops (tubers), according to the *Oxford Book of Food Plants*. In macrobiotic cooking, since root crops are considered vegetables, vegetables are the primary side dishes served with grains.

Along with fruits, vegetables are the perishable foods. They live only during their seasons and are not natural "keepers" like grains and beans which store easily year-round. The selection and preparation of **seasonal** produce, grown as **locally** as possible, are practices which heighten our awareness of natural order. By eating foods which survive the changing seasons in or close to our area, we strengthen our ability to survive there as well.

"Locally grown" may mean the backyard **garden**, the greatest teacher for understanding the cycles of nature through planting, tending, and harvesting. You can even grow vegetable varieties which rarely appear in any market. A number of high quality seed companies now print fascinating catalogs, full of information both historic and practical.

Local might be the countryside around town where produce is grown for farmer's markets or local food stores. Or, in its broadest sense, local means within the same climatic zone. So, for most of us who live in the temperate zone, foods from that area are appropriate for us.

There are probably more ways to cook vegetables than any other food. Cooking brings out the best qualities of vegetables—their digestibility, color, and taste. Cooking breaks up tough fibers and makes the nutrients more available. Cooking also sanitizes vegetables so they become human food devoid of bacteria from the soil, a fact the Chinese people honor to this day. They even cook sprouts by passing a strainer full of them through a pot of boiling water.

The possible balance of textures to be achieved in preparing vegetables is truly exciting—from crisp and crunchy raw or pressed salads and quick pickles to quick-boiled or steamed vegetables, on to the lightly sautéed, long-time baked or pressure cooked vegetables, thoroughly softened for soups and sauces. Each cooking technique imparts its own quality. Leftover vegetables are the ideal snack food and their cooking broths make delicious beverages. As one bright hue or in colorful combination, vegetable dishes should be beautiful.

For information on sea vegetables, see page 59.

Sautéing

Very little oil is used in the macrobiotic approach to cooking. Many people enjoy one lightly sautéed dish per day or per meal, served along with another vegetable dish which has been simmered, steamed, boiled, or baked. When you consider how oil is made, it becomes a very special food. Many seeds are crushed by machinery under enormous pressure to extract the oil. If we had to do this ourselves, how precious oil would be! People cooking to regain their health often limit their oil intake to just two times per week. A little more oil is used in winter than in summer cooking as it helps produce body heat.

A little oil goes a long way. Nutritionally speaking it's about 100 percent fat. Even though it is a vegetable quality food and the fat is unsaturated, it is still fat. We use oil in cooking for enhancing the flavor of a dish and to facilitate cooking. Oil attracts heat so when vegetables are lightly tossed in a heated, oiled pan, this thin coating acts to conduct heat, thus helping to cook the vegetable quickly.

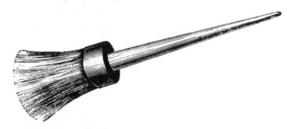

Keep a pastry brush in a cup by the stove. For sautéing vegetables or to coat a baking sheet or dish, pour in a little oil, then brush it over the cooking surface so it's well distributed. Any excess can be poured off into the cup. Wash cup and brush weekly.

Sesame oil is light with a fine, delicate taste, ideal for daily vegetable cookery. Toasted sesame oil is dark. It adds an irresistible quality to the flavor and aroma of a dish and is used occasionally. Olive oil adds authenticity to Italian dishes. Corn oil is mostly used for baking since its bright color and rich texture resemble butter, and because it comes from grain like the flours with which it is prepared in breads and pastries. Other nut and seed oils, such as sunflower, safflower, etc., may be used as well.

Look for oils which have a lot of color and a rich, thick texture. The Arrowhead Mills brand fills this requirement for quality. Hold a jar up to the same type of oil under another label and compare the difference.

Sautéed vegetables may be prepared with or without the addition of water, or even oil. (See the simmer or water sauté method which follows.) For long, slow cooking in a covered pot, even with bigger pieces, no extra water is needed as the natural juices in the vegetables will come out. But for quicker cooking over moderate or high heat, as when you're in a hurry or for stir-frying, a little water is added to thinly cut vegetables to prevent sticking or burning. When done, there should be next to no liquid left in the pot, but if there is, simply pour it off and set aside for use in soup.

A little sea salt added early in cooking brings out the vegetable juices, but is optional. I usually omit it. Season vegetable dishes with good quality soy sauce in the last few minutes of cooking.

Seasonal Vegetable Sauté

Serves 3

1 teaspoon sesame oil
1 onion or equivalent amount other onion family member (leeks, green onions, shallots), sliced thin
2 carrots, or 1 carrot and equal amount of other root vegetable or squash, cut in thin diagonals or half-moons
2 cups leafy greens in season (kale, cabbage, bok choy, collard or mustard greens, etc.), sliced thin
½ cup water (optional)
1 tablespoon good quality soy sauce, or to taste

Lightly brush skillet with oil. Heat oil, then sauté onion briefly. Add root vegetables and stir to coat with oil.

Cook without water, slowly over low heat, covered, until root vegetables are halfway done before adding greens. Or to cook more quickly at a higher temperature, add water and cook over medium-low to medium heat.

Drizzle soy sauce over vegetables in last few minutes and stir once before serving.

For large amounts, multiply ingredients, except water which should be one inch deep in pot.

Sea Palm Sauté

Serves 2-4
Makes 2 cups

Sea palm is a wild California sea vegetable which grows in the cold waters off the north coast. It is one of the mildest tasting sea vegetables. For this reason, and because it's so easy to soak and cook, sea palm is ideal to serve to newcomers to the world of sea vegetables.

½ cup dry sea palm
2 cups water
1 teaspoon sesame oil
1 medium onion, cut in ¼ inch slices
1 medium carrot, cut in ¼ inch matchsticks
1 tablespoon good quality soy sauce
1 tablespoon green onion, chives, or parsley, cut in thin diagonals or minced for garnish

Soak sea palm in water until reconstituted, about 15 minutes. Meanwhile, cut vegetables, heat oil, and sauté onion and carrot briefly.

Cut sea palm fronds in three-inch pieces and mince stem end. Push vegetables to side of pan and place soaked sea palm on bottom, then place vegetables on top of sea palm. Add soaking water to barely cover the sea palm, taking care to avoid using the last bit of water where sand or other particles may have settled.

Bring to boil, then simmer covered for 20 minutes. Add soy sauce and leave cover off to cook away any extra liquid, about 10 minutes more. Or, to serve immediately, pour off and reserve any liquid that remains, add soy sauce, and stir once before serving, garnished.

Vegetable Sauté with Ume-Kuzu Sauce

Serves 6

1 tablespoon toasted sesame oil
1 onion, sliced in thin crescents
1 cup carrot
1 cup celery
4 cups broccoli
½ cup green onion tops, cut in 2 inch slices
2 cups cool water
2 tablespoons pickled plum *(umeboshi)* vinegar
¼ cup *kuzu* root starch
1 teaspoon sesame seeds, toasted for garnish

Cut carrot in thin diagonals and celery in slightly larger diagonals. Cut off one or two inches of hard broccoli bottom stem and discard. Cut top part in half crosswise, then cut in flowerettes. Cut hard skin off midsection and slice lengthwise.

Heat oil and sauté onion briefly. Mix *ume* vinegar and water in a separate bowl. Layer vegetables over onions, except green onions, and pour one-half cup *ume*-water mixture over. Mix *kuzu* with remaining liquid.

Bring vegetables to boil, then slow boil, covered, until vegetables are soft, around 10 minutes.

Stir *kuzu* mixture and pour over vegetables. Add green onions. Stir gently as sauce thickens and liquid becomes clear. Garnish to serve.

Summer's End Vegetable Dish

Serves 8

Adopted from a Hopi recipe (see book mentioned on page 23), the ingredients are perfectly suited for late summer. Although people with arthritis and other joint pain problems are advised not to eat the nightshade family of vegetables (tomato, potato, eggplant, and all peppers except black pepper; see page 80), healthy people enjoy them on occasion when they are in their short season. In most temperate areas, the months of August and September are those times. Of course, potatoes store well, extending their season.

Use double the amount of green beans if you can't find fresh limas, and leave out the chili pepper if desired, although the Anaheim is reportedly one of the mildest hot peppers.

   1 tablespoon corn oil
   1 onion
   1 clove garlic, minced
  ½ small green Anaheim chili pepper
     (optional)
   1 sweet red pepper (or part green bell
     pepper)
   1 cup fresh lima beans (1 pound in pod)
   1 cup green beans (¼ pound), cut in 1 inch
     pieces
   1 pound summer squash (patty pan and
     yellow crookneck), 1 quart cut
   4 ears corn
   1 teaspoon sea salt
  ¼ cup water
   2 teaspoons fresh sage, minced

To cut corn kernels from cobs, hold corn in a bowl and cut downwards, then scrape upwards to extract the flavorful juice. Dice onion, pepper, and summer squash in one-half inch cubes.

Heat oil and add all ingredients, except corn. Bring to boil, then simmer covered 10 minutes. Add corn, stir well, and cook 10 minutes more.

Works well simply multiplied for large quantities.

Mung Bean Threads with Chinese Cabbage and Mushrooms

Serves 4

   1 ounce mung bean threads
   4 dried *shiitake* mushrooms
   4 cups water
   1 teaspoon sesame oil
   1 cup leeks, cut in ½ inch diagonals
   4 cups Chinese cabbage, quarter whole
     cabbage lengthwise, then cut in ½ inch
     slices across
  ¼ cup mushroom cooking broth
   1 tablespoon good quality soy sauce

Place threads with mushrooms and water in pot and bring to boil. Remove pan from stove immediately, cover, and let sit for 10 minutes. Drain liquid, reserving one-quarter cup for further cooking. Run cool water over bean threads in strainer and set aside. Cut off and discard mushroom stems and slice tops.

Heat oil and sauté leeks briefly, add sliced mushrooms, Chinese cabbage, and one-quarter cup soaking liquid. Bring to boil, then cook covered until crispy soft, about eight minutes.

Cut bean threads in two-inch lengths and gently mix into vegetables. Sprinkle with soy sauce and cover to heat through, about two minutes longer. For large amounts, for example 60 people, increase all ingredients proportionately except oil and water, which should be increased only by half.

Simmering

For oil-free vegetable dishes, all the sautéed vegetable recipes may be prepared by substituting a little water for the oil. This method is also known as water sautéing.

Umeboshi Cabbage

Serves 3-4

These tangy simmered greens are always popular. The taste is delicious and the possible combinations are almost endless. It's a great way to introduce the use of the pickled plum *(umeboshi)* as an alternative, healthful seasoning in your cuisine. See page 79 for more information.

> 4 cups cabbage (about ½ head), sliced
> 1 cup bright green vegetables, optional for variety (watercress, kale, collard, etc.) sliced
> ½ cup water
> 2 pickled plums *(umeboshi)*, pitted, or 1 tablespoon *ume* paste

Rub plums on bottom of pan and reserve pits, or use *ume* paste. Add water and vegetables. Cover pan, bring to boil, then simmer until done, about 10 minutes. Mix to serve.

For large amounts, barely cover bottom of pan with water since so much liquid comes out of the vegetables.

Miso Carrot Tops

Serves 3

A nice way to take your miso, cooked in with vegetables instead of soup. This dish, using the whole carrot, has a surprisingly pleasant, sweet taste.

> 1 onion, cut in thin crescents
> 2 carrots, roots cut in thin diagonals and tops minced
> ⅓ cup water
> 2 level tablespoons miso (barley is nice)

Layer onion, then carrots, then carrot tops in pan. Pour water over, cover, bring to boil, then simmer until done, about 15 minutes. Dissolve miso in hot cooking broth, stir into vegetables and cook two minutes longer.

Steaming

Steaming is a simple way to appreciate vegetables for their own honest flavors. Any steamer is fine—the stainless steel, fold-up variety available in most hardware/kitchen stores, or a pot specifically designed with holes in the bottom for steaming over another pot of water. My favorite is the Chinese steamer basket. Made of bamboo, these baskets stack so that many dishes may be cooked over one heat source, saving valuable fuel. Place the bamboo steamer over a pan of water which is slightly larger at the rim than

the steamer to prevent it from burning if the flame is high. To cook vegetables which are cut smaller than the spaces between the steamer slats, lay down moistened cheesecloth first. Bamboo steamers are so nice looking they make attractive serving containers. Save steaming liquid for soups, sauces, or for a refreshing beverage. See the section entitled *Garnishes and Flavor Enhancers for Steamed or Boiled Vegetables* on the following page.

Steamed Greens with Carrot Flowers / Steamed Kohlrabi Bulbs and Greens

These two general recipes are listed together and without ingredient amounts because they are prepared in the same way. The cooking technique is simple, free of any salt, oil, or seasoning.

> Any greens (mustard, kale, collard, etc.),
> sliced; or, halved Brussels sprouts;
> or kohlrabi, bulbs sliced in ¼ inch half
> moons, leaves cut in ¼ inch slices
> Flower-cut carrots, thinly sliced
> Water to steam

Place vegetables in steamer basket and set in place. Bring water to boil and cook covered until done, about 8-10 minutes. Reserve cooking liquid for use as soup base or to enjoy as a tasty refreshing beverage in place of tea or water.

Sweet and Sour Broccoli and Onions with Wheatmeat

Serves 4-5

> 4 cups broccoli, cut in long flowerettes
> 1 small onion, cut in ½ inch crescents
> ½ cup wheatmeat, sliced thin
> 1½ cups *Chinese Red Sweet and Sour Sauce*

Chinese Red Sweet and Sour Sauce:

Makes 1½ cups

> 1 tablespoon pickled plum *(umeboshi)*
> vinegar
> ¼ cup brown rice syrup
> 2 tablespoons rice vinegar
> 1 cup cool water
> ¼ cup *Red Sauce*
> 1 heaping tablespoon *kuzu* root starch

Red Sauce:

Makes 1⅔ cups

> 1½ cups carrots
> 1 small beet
> ½ cup water

Prepare wheatmeat (see page 40).

To prepare *Red Sauce*, cut vegetables in one-inch chunks and pressure cook with water for five minutes. Puree in blender.

Steam broccoli and onions together until tender, about 8-10 minutes.

While vegetables cook, prepare *Sweet and Sour Sauce*. Place all ingredients in saucepan and stir to dissolve *kuzu*. Turn heat high and stir while mixture comes to boil to avoid lumping. Mixture will turn a shiny, red color.

Mix gently with cooked vegetables to serve.

Boiling

Boiling is another easy, healthful cooking technique which brings out the vivid colors in vegetables. Boiling is quicker than steaming because the vegetable is completely immersed in the hot liquid. Vegetables may be simply boiled in water, or in lightly salted water to retain minerals and flavor. Figure one-half teaspoon sea salt per quart water. Or boil vegetables in a stock which becomes richer in flavor as the ingredients release some of their juices in cooking. Quickly boiled vegetables retain the most nutrients.

The cooking broths make wonderful soup or sauce stocks, or beverages. The only broths not to use are those from bitter tasting vegetables such as dandelion or mustard greens.

Bring water to boil over high heat. Boil vegetables with the lid on to guard against evaporation and to allow for even distribution of heat. To eliminate time-consuming cutting, whole green leaves may be cooked and then drained and cooled slightly before being chopped fine. The volume will be much less after boiling.

Garnishes and Flavor Enhancers for Steamed or Boiled Vegetables

Boiled vegetables have a clear, clean flavor of their own which can be highlighted in the same ways as steamed vegetables.

• A few **flower-cut carrots**, thinly sliced, may be laid on top to cook with greens, providing a colorful garnish when served.

• **Toasted sunflower, pumpkin, or sesame seeds** may be sprinkled over the vegetables in the serving bowl. Crush and mix them with toasted and crushed sea vegetable flakes for variety. Seeds become soggy if cooked with the vegetables.

• It's worthwhile to learn how to prepare a variety of **dressings** and **sauces** ranging from easy to fancy. A simple sprinkling of **pickled plum** *(ume)* **vinegar, rice vinegar,** or equal parts **lemon, lime juice, or vinegar and soy sauce** will dress up any vegetable dish. For prepared sauces, see pages 79 through 81, and the sauces listing in the index.

Boiled Greens with Toasted Pumpkin Seeds

Serves 2
Makes 1½ cups

1 quart (4 cups) whole green leaves
    (kale, collard, mustard, bok choy, etc.),
    well packed
1½ quarts (6 cups) water
  ¾ teaspoon sea salt (optional)
  2 tablespoons pumpkin (or sunflower or
    sesame) seeds, toasted and sprinkled
    with good quality soy sauce

Fold greens in half and stuff into container to measure. Bring (salted) water to boil. Rinse greens and add whole to boiling water. Greens should be completely submerged.

Return to boil and slow boil, covered, until done, about five minutes.

Drain and allow to cool slightly or quickly rinse greens under cool water if you need to handle them quickly. Squeeze out excess liquid and cut as desired. Fluff greens if compacted and toss with seeds.

Recipe works perfectly doubled; for larger amounts, decrease water by at least half and boil greens in several batches.

Boiled Onions and Mixed Greens with Sunflower Sprinkles

A nice way to use leftover greens.

  Mixed greens
1 small onion, cut in crescents
2 tablespoons sunflower seeds, toasted and
    sprinkled with good quality soy sauce

Cook greens as above, then boil onion until done, about five minutes. Toss vegetables with seeds to serve.

Corn on the Cob with Umeboshi

What is there to do with fresh-cooked corn except drown it in butter and raw salt? A surprisingly delicious alternative is the pickled *umeboshi* plum (see page 79). Figure up to one plum per person depending on size, or tear plums in quarters or halves to serve with fresh corn.

    4 ears corn
      Water
  2-4 pickled plums

To prepare corn, husk and scrub with vegetable brush quickly and gently to remove silk, and add to boiling water to cook for about five minutes.

Just rub the plum over cooked corn for a new taste sensation you'll want to repeat all corn season long.

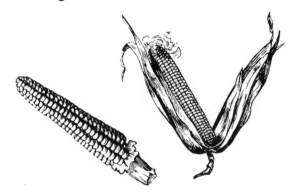

Stand-Up Cabbage Sushi

Serves 4

Makes 8 two-inch or 16 one-inch slices

This seasoned vegetable roll is a sushi without rice. An ideal finger food. For added color, include a thin carrot strip in filling.

    4 large or 8 small cabbage leaves
    4 dark greens (mustard, kale, or
        equivalent volume of watercress)
    2 quarts (8 cups) water
    2 teaspoons rice vinegar, pickled plum *(ume)*
        vinegar, or good quality soy sauce
    1 teaspoon brown or black sesame seeds,
        toasted

Cut off cabbage bottom, then separate whole leaves. Cut out hard bottom center part of leaves. Bring water to boil, then add leaves and cook until done, about five minutes. Remove to a towel to dry and cool. Boil whole dark greens until done, about two to five minutes (less for watercress). Remove to a towel to dry and cool. Squeeze excess liquid from dark greens and sprinkle with vinegar.

Spread cabbage leaves out flat and layer one on top of the other. Lay dark greens across bottom edge of cabbage and roll up tightly. You should end up with two one-and-one-half-inch thick rolls. Now cut sushi into one-inch or two-inch pieces and stand them up so you can view the colorful spiral within. Sprinkle with seeds to serve.

For a different shape, cut roll in half and then cut each half on the diagonal. Stand sushi up on flat side.

For large amounts decrease cooking water by half.

Glazed Red Radishes

Serves 3-4

Foremost macrobiotic cooking teacher Aveline Kushi demonstrated this strikingly beautiful dish in one of her classes. Another way to serve an *ume-kuzu* sauce (see *Vegetable Sauté with Ume-Kuzu Sauce* recipe, page 51).

- 1 cup (about 1 bunch or ½ pound) red radishes, rinsed, greens removed and radishes trimmed
- 1 tablespoon pickled *umeboshi* plum paste (or about 1-2 plums)
- ½ cup water
- 1 level tablespoon *kuzu* root starch

Tear off pieces of plum (if used) and place on bottom of saucepan, reserving pits in a jar to use later (see page 64). Add radishes and most of the water. Bring to boil, then simmer 10 minutes. Dissolve kuzu in remaining cool water and add to saucepan. Stir to spread color and flavor, and watch the bright shiny red sauce appear. No garnish needed.

New England Boiled Dinner with Wheatmeat

Serves 4

In this adaptation of an early American favorite, soy sauce simulates the mildly salty flavor and the color of meat stock, and oil fulfills the rich quality. Incredibly delicious!

Stock:
- 2 quarts (8 cups) water
- 2 tablespoons good quality soy sauce
- 1 tablespoon corn oil
- 1 teaspoon dry thyme or 1 sprig fresh
- 1 teaspoon dry marjoram or 1 sprig fresh

Vegetables:
- 1 onion, quartered
- 2 small carrots, halved
- ½ turnip or rutabaga, quartered
- 4 wedges cabbage (½ head cut in 6 wedges)
- 1 cup wheatmeat, cut in 8 chunks
- ¼ cup parsley, chopped for garnish

Prepare wheatmeat (see page 40).

Bring stock ingredients to boil in covered pot. Add onion, carrot, and turnip or rutabaga. Return to boil, then simmer 10 minutes. Add cabbage, return to boil, then turn flame low to simmer 10 minutes more. Remove vegetables carefully to retain their shape.

Reheat wheatmeat by bringing it to boil in its own stock or by adding it to this stock for a minute. Reserve stock(s) for soup or sauce base at future meal.

To serve, place one wedge of each vegetable on each plate. Add two wheatmeat chunks per serving; garnish all with a sprinkling of parsley.

For large amounts, decrease stock ingredients by half.

Vegetable Casserole and Pie

Green Corn Tamale Bake

Serves 8

"Green corn" is another name for fresh corn off the cob. This dish uses both fresh and dried corn (flour) in a combination that has wonderful flavor and texture.

    3 cups winter squash puree
    1 tablespoon corn oil
    1 onion, diced
    1 bell pepper, diced
    2 cloves garlic, minced
    2 cups fresh corn kernels (2 large or 4 small ears)
    2 tablespoons good quality soy sauce
    ½ cup cornmeal

To make squash puree, either bake whole squash at 450 degrees until soft, about one hour, or cut squash in two-inch chunks and pressure cook five minutes with one cup water, or steam or boil squash until done. Remove skin and seeds. Mash and measure.

Heat oil and sauté onion, pepper, and garlic. Add remaining ingredients and mix well. When mixture is heated throughout, spoon into corn-oiled one-quart casserole, baking dish, or pie pan and bake covered for one-half hour at 350 degrees, then uncovered for one-half hour more.

Sunshine Pie

Serves 8

A vegetable pie in a whole millet crust, the original version appeared in the *East West Journal Cooklet* (now out-of-print) years ago. Sunshine Pie gets its name from the colorful combination of a golden yellow crust with a splash of bright orange for filling.

Whole Millet Crust:
    ½ cup millet
    1½ cups water
    ⅛ teaspoon sea salt

Vegetable Puree:
    2 quarts rutabaga (or other orange vegetable such as carrot or winter squash — butternut, sweetmeat, or other variety), cut in 1 inch chunks
    1 cup water

Filling:
    3 cups vegetable puree
    ½ cup cooking broth
    ¼ cup agar sea vegetable flakes
    1½ teaspoons good quality soy sauce
    1½ teaspoons *ume* vinegar
    1 tablespoon sunflower seeds, lightly toasted and sprinkled with soy sauce, for garnish

To prepare crust, boil rinsed millet in salted water for one-half hour. No flame spreader necessary. Press hot millet into corn-oiled pie plate with a moistened rubber spatula, then fingers. Bake 20 minutes at 350 degrees.

To prepare vegetable puree, bring rutabaga and water to pressure and cook 15 minutes. (Other vegetables may need just five minutes of pressure cooking.) Puree while hot. Drain and set aside cooking broth.

To assemble filling, first bring cooking broth and agar to boil in small saucepan and simmer until agar completely dissolves, about two minutes. Mix well with puree and seasonings and spoon into prebaked pie shell. Garnish and allow to gel, about one-and-one-half hours at room temperature.

Sea Vegetables

Sea vegetables are becoming a very important feature in natural foods cookery because of their delicious new flavors and incredible amount and variety of nutrients. Macrobiotic cookbooks are a good way to find ways of preparing them. Most other sea vegetable recipes contain undesirable ingredients such as sugar and large amounts of oil, but they can be good sources for ideas. Because most of us are unaccustomed to eating sea vegetables, it's best to start with small portions, one to two tablespoons dry, of the mild varieties (arame, sea palm, and wakame). Then gradually increase the amount and variety to allow the taste buds and intestinal flora to adjust to the new food. Sea vegetables act like miso in developing enzymes and thereby restoring health to the intestines. You'll be surprised to find that sea vegetables don't taste salty, being only two to eight percent salt. They don't really taste fishy either, although that's what some people expect.

Before long, you'll be making sure you include a sea vegetable in one dish at every meal, and planning about two meals a week where they take their place as a vegetable dish.

All it takes to prepare sea vegetables is an initial soaking of 10 to 20 minutes, so they fully soften and expand, and then cutting into smaller pieces for cooking. These steps are not necessary when using sea vegetables in soups or beans where you may simply add the dry sea vegetable to the pot. In this book, sea vegetables are cooked with beans, in soups, salads, as a side dish, as a table seasoning, in trail mix, wrapped around rice, and to make gels and aspics.

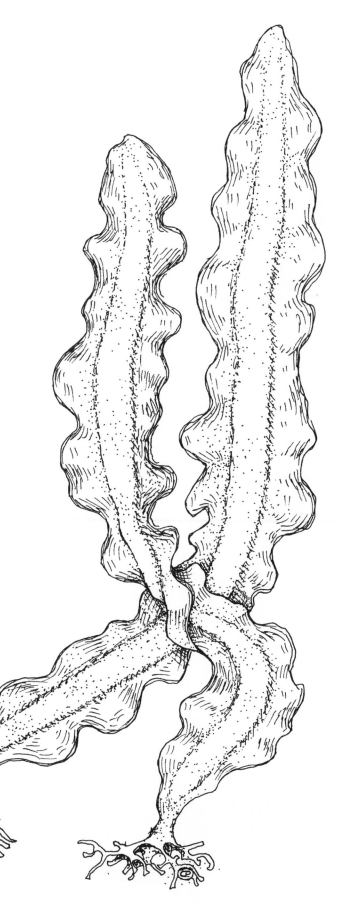

Salads

Salads add depth and a seemingly endless variety of colors, flavors, and textures to the grain and vegetable chef's repertoire. They may be as simple as just three ingredients with a single seasoning or a more elaborate and subtle combination of several ingredients and flavor enhancers. Either way, salads can provide a clearly stated main dish or the small accent of a side dish.

As people who have eaten a lot of animal food in the recent past, North Americans enjoy salads often and even crave them. This may be an instinctive way to lighten up and let go of past accumulations of fat and toxins on our way to more balanced staple fare.

Salads are to be enjoyed year-round. The crisp, cool quality of summer salads satisfies the need for nourishment that refreshes. During cooler months, lightly boiled or steamed and dressed vegetables continue to fulfill the desire for the crisp-tender texture. These types of dishes are known as boiled, cooked, hot, or winter salads.

Sea vegetables become a tasty focus at a meal when simply prepared, combined with lightly cooked or raw land vegetables, and nicely dressed. Many people who would otherwise avoid sea vegetables become enamored of them in salads.

Whole grain noodles are light grains which are easy to digest since they are boiled soft instead of baked dry and firm like crackers or some breads. Cool noodles are ideal salad ingredients which lend themselves to many types of dressings.

It's all in the sauce! Well, not quite . . . salad ingredients must be properly prepared and combined, which can only be learned by experience. But the final touch is the accent which highlights the dish, be it a sprig of parsley or a delicious salad dressing.

Macrobiotics has brought many high quality foods and seasonings to the attention of North Americans. Little by little, they are being prepared here in the U.S. with local ingredients. When combined with or substituted for ingredients we already use, the results are exciting—better health and a new range of creative possibilities.

Rice vinegar (brown or white rice) has a gentler flavor and aroma than apple cider or wine vinegars. Perhaps this is due to its origin in grains instead of fruits.

The pickled *umeboshi* plum, or *ume* for short, comes in three forms: the whole plum, plum paste, and plum liquid called *umeboshi* vinegar. *Ume* vinegar enhances the acid quality of regular vinegars with the alkalinizing effect of the pickled plum. This makes it an ideal food for people who are restoring their health.

Good quality soy sauce or miso combine well with lemon or lime juice or rice vinegar for simple, yet superb, oil-free dressings.

Creamy dressings are made with seasoned fresh tofu. For more information on tofu, see page 74.

Agar sea vegetable flakes are used like gelatin to make aspics or gelled salads. For more information on agar, see page 69.

Unforgettable dressings are made with seed and nut "butters" or high-quality oils. Utilizing whole seeds and nuts is a better way to enjoy the richness of oil than machine-pressed oils. Seed and nut butters contain the whole food, simply toasted and crushed, so all the fiber and balanced nutrients are intact.

With the commercial availability of quality

peanut, sesame, almond, and sunflower butters, and of sesame tahini (hulled sesame seed paste), a whole new world of dressing possibilities opens up. A simple hand mill with steel grinding plates enables one to make nut and seed butters with other lightly toasted, temperate climate varieties such as pumpkin seeds, hazelnuts (also called filberts), pecans, and walnuts.

For variety, use both nut and seed butters and good quality oils. Take pleasure in the musty Italian flavor and aroma only associated with olive oil, or the enticing quality of toasted sesame oil always used in good Oriental cooking.

Amazing dressings are created with these simple ingredients. The possibilities are expanded with the addition of small amounts of herbs, onion, garlic, ginger, and mustard.

Because of oil's high fat content and refined nature, only a small amount for sautéing is recommended for people using diet to aid in their recovery from illness. See page 50 for more information on oil. When serving people who choose not to eat certain dressing ingredients, take care of them by preparing several undressed salads. Give them a choice of *ume* vinegar for all types of salads and/or sesame salt for whole grain or noodle salads.

Whole Grain- or Noodle-Vegetable Salads

Holly's Rice Salad with Herb Vinaigrette Dressing

Serves 4

Fit for a wedding, this whole grain and vegetable salad was served at ours, made by Holly Blackwood herself. At summer camp, where some people choose not to eat these dressing ingredients for health reasons, I left several salads undressed and served *ume* vinegar and sesame salt on the side.

4 cups cooked short grain brown rice, firmly packed
½ cup cooked chickpeas (garbanzo beans)
½ cup each carrot, celery, cauliflower, green onions, and parsley
¼ cup almonds, toasted
½ small head soft green lettuce (bibb, oak, or green leaf)
½ cup *Herb Vinaigrette Dressing*

Herb Vinaigrette Dressing:

Makes ½ cup

¼ cup sesame oil
¼ cup rice vinegar
1 clove garlic, minced
1 tablespoon good quality soy sauce
½ teaspoon basil
½ teaspoon oregano

To prepare chickpeas which are digestible yet firm enough to hold their shape in a salad, see page 75 and decrease cooking time to one-half hour.

Dice carrot and celery to size of beans. Break cauliflower into tiny flowerettes. Slice green onion and parsley thin. Steam carrot, celery, and cauliflower until done and allow to cool.

Prepare dressing by mixing ingredients well.

Pour dressing over rice in large serving bowl. Work in well. Add remaining ingredients, reserving a tiny amount of each to set on top. Mix well with open fingers to avoid breaking cooked vegetables. Arrange lettuce leaves around outside edge of salad.

Works well for large amounts.

Spiral Noodle Salad with Tofu Green Goddess Dressing

Serves 3
Makes 5 cups

4 cups sesame rice spirals (little less than
    ½ pound) or other pasta
2 quarts water
½ cup carrots, cut in thin half moon slices
½ cup cauliflower (or sunchoke), separated
    into small flowerettes, or diced
½ cup onion, diced
½ cup red cabbage, sliced thin
½ cup sunflower seeds, toasted and sprinkled
    with soy sauce
¼ cup parsley, chopped
1½ cup *Tofu Green Goddess Dressing*

Tofu Green Goddess Dressing:
Makes 1½ cups
½ pound tofu, soft and fresh
2 tablespoons good quality soy sauce
2 tablespoons rice vinegar
1 cup parsley, chopped
¼ cup water

Bring water to boil and add noodles. Cook until done, about 10 minutes. Strain noodles, reserving hot cooking liquid, then run noodles under cold water, drain, and set aside to cool. Return enough water to pot for use in boiling tofu for dressing.

Steam carrots and cauliflower until crispy-soft, about five minutes, and remove to cool. Steam onion and red cabbage about three minutes and cool. Mix noodles and vegetables. Toss with seeds and parsley just before serving to retain crisp textures.

To prepare *Tofu Green Goddess Dressing*, boil tofu five minutes, drain, and allow to cool. Blend remaining ingredients, then crumble in tofu and blend until creamy smooth. For large amounts, start with no water and add it as needed.

Pour dressing over salad or serve it at the side.

Japanese Cool Noodle Salad

Serves 3-6

Thanks to Diane Bitte. This salad was the hit of the day at our summer camp picnic by the river.

1 8.8 ounce package whole wheat *jinenjo*
    noodles (or other kind)
6 dried *shiitake* mushrooms
1 small cucumber, cut in thin matchsticks,
    or 1 cup celery, cut in thin diagonals
1 cup carrots, cut in thin matchsticks
½ cup green onion tops, sliced in thin
    diagonals
    Little less than 1 cup *Sesame Seed
    Dressing*

Sesame Seed Dressing:
Makes a little less than 1 cup
¼ cup sesame seeds, toasted
¼ cup *shiitake* mushroom cooking broth
¼ cup good quality soy sauce
2 tablespoons rice vinegar
1 tablespoon toasted sesame oil
1 tablespoon sweet rice wine *(mirin)*,
    optional
1 tablespoon ginger, fresh grated

Cook noodles (about eight minutes for jinenjo), then drain and cool by running under cool water.

Bring mushrooms to boil in water to cover and simmer until soft, about 10 to 20 minutes. Add carrot (and celery if used) in last three minutes to cook slightly. Drain, reserving broth for dressing. Cut off mushroom stems and discard, then cut tops in thin slices.

Divide noodles into three to six portions and place in individual serving bowls. Place clusters of each vegetable in separate mounds atop noodles. To serve large groups, mix all ingredients together.

Prepare dressing by grinding toasted seeds until three-fourths are ground up. Mix with other ingredients.

Pour dressing over salads to serve.

Land and Sea Vegetable Salads

Cucumber-Wakame Salad with Vinegar-Soy Sauce Dressing

Serves 3
Makes 2¼ cups

1 cup cucumber (1 small cuke), sliced in
   thin rounds
¼ cup wakame sea vegetable, well packed
1 cup water
½ cup alfalfa sprouts (or red radishes, sliced
   in thin rounds, or flower-cut carrots,
   steamed or boiled)
1 tablespoon sesame seeds, toasted for
   garnish
2 tablespoons *Vinegar-Soy Sauce Dressing*

Vinegar-Soy Sauce Dressing:
1 tablespoon rice vinegar (or lemon or lime
   juice)
1 tablespoon good quality soy sauce (or
   miso)

To measure wakame, roll up a dry strip and stuff
into measuring cup. Soak wakame in water
(halve amount of water for large volume) until
reconstituted, about five minutes, and lay out on
cutting board. Cut out hard midrib and save for
use in soups. Cut main portion in one-inch
squares. Cook in water to cover until tender but
not mushy, about one to five minutes. Gently
mix ingredients. Mix dressing ingredients and
dress to serve. Garnish if desired.

Arame-Broccoli Salad with Light Plum-Parsley Dressing

Serves 4

Ume vinegar is a simple oil-free substitute for
the dressing in this recipe. The dressing is based
on a delicious broth you can make at home with
the pickled plum *(umeboshi)* pits.

½ cup arame sea vegetable
3 cups broccoli
6 cups water (2 cups to soak arame, 4 cups
   to cook broccoli)
⅛ teaspoon sea salt
½ small head green leaf lettuce
½ cup *Light Plum-Parsley Dressing*, or
   2 tablespoons *ume* vinegar
1 teaspoon carrot, grated for garnish

Light Plum-Parsley Dressing:
Makes 1¼ cups
1 cup *Pickled Plum (Ume) Pit Broth*
1 tablespoon *ume* paste
¼ cup parsley, chopped and well packed
¼ cup nut butter (almond, sesame, etc.)
1 clove garlic (optional)

Pickled Plum (Ume) Pit Broth:
Makes a little less than 1 cup
1 cup water
10 plum pits

Soak arame in two cups water just until reconstituted, about 10 minutes. Drain arame, reserving
liquid for plants.

Meanwhile, trim bottom of broccoli stems
and cut crosswise at three-inch intervals from
top. Cut lengthwise in half-inch sections so
flowerettes stay together. Bring four cups salted
water to boil, add broccoli, and cook covered
until crisp-soft, about five minutes. Drain and
set aside to cool. Return water to boil, add
drained arame and boil for one minute. Drain,
reserving broth to use in soups, etc., and set
arame aside to cool, or hasten the process by
running quickly under cool water.

To assemble salad, tear rinsed lettuce into
salad bowl. Layer broccoli over arame, placing
stems under flowerettes, and leaving a small
green border of lettuce around the outside.

To prepare broth for dressing, bring water
and pits to boil, then slow boil covered for 10
minutes. Strain and allow to cool.

To make dressing, blend ingredients until smooth. Should you decide not to make the broth, substitute one cup water and one tablespoon more *ume* paste.

Dress salad and garnish with grated carrot to serve.

Dulse-Sprout Salad with Lemon-Poppy Seed Dressing

Serves 4-5

1 cup mixed sprouts (mung, azuki, chickpea, green pea)
1 cup alfalfa sprouts
4 large lettuce leaves
¼ cup dulse sea vegetable, gently packed
6 tablespoons *Lemon-Poppy Seed Dressing*

Lemon-Poppy Seed Dressing:

Makes 6 tablespoons

2 tablespoons light miso
2 tablespoons lemon or lime juice (or combination)
¼ cup water
¼ teaspoon poppy seeds

Bring a small saucepan of water to boil and add mixed sprouts and cook for one minute. Drain and cool. Do not cook alfalfa sprouts. Tear lettuce into bite-size pieces and mix with both kinds of sprouts.

Soak dulse in water to cover for about 30 seconds and look and feel to see that no hard particles are attached to the surface or within the folds. Tear into small pieces and toss with other salad ingredients.

Mix dressing ingredients and dress to serve.

Boiled Salads

Boiled salads can be served warm, at room temperature, or cooled. It's fun to choose vegetables for a balanced display of colors and textures. Light and dark greens, such as bok choy with kale or cabbage with watercress, are beautifully accented with bright orange carrots, yellow rutabagas, and the creamy parsnip hue.

Bring salted water (one-half teaspoon sea salt per quart water) to boil. It isn't necessary to salt the water, but salt keeps some nutrients and flavor from leaching into the water, and also adds taste. Cook vegetables until crispy-soft. Light vegetables such as watercress and sprouts (all but alfalfa sprouts, which lose their pleasant texture when cooked) may just be dipped in boiling water for a few seconds. Most other vegetables cook in one to five minutes after water resumes boiling, depending on the type and how they are cut. Greens and grated or thinly-sliced or matchstick-cut vegetables cook quicker than carrots or turnips cut in larger slices.

Strain and set aside to cool or serve immediately, as is or garnished. Toss or sprinkle with lightly toasted sunflower, pumpkin, sesame, or poppy seeds, or with minced parsley and/or a dressing. Any salad dressing in this chapter may be used for boiled salads as well. For distinct colors, cluster together each vegetable and arrange side by side on a leaf or bed of lettuce.

Composed Boiled Salad with Ume Vinegar

Serves 5

A composed salad has its ingredients served in an arranged fashion rather than tossed together.

  6 cups bok choy or other greens
  1 cup carrot
  ½ cup burdock, turnip, or daikon radish
1½ cups onion
  ¼ cup green onion tops
  2 quarts water
  1 teaspoon sea salt (optional)
  1 tablespoon *ume* vinegar

Cut large bok choy leaves down center, then cut both large and small leaves in quarter-inch slices. Cut carrot and burdock in very thin diagonals. Cut onion in thin crescents and green onion tops in two-inch slices.

  Bring (salted) water to boil. Add bok choy and cook until crispy soft, about two minutes. Strain out to cool, then add carrot to cook about four minutes and remove. Add onion to cook for five minutes and remove, then green onion (two minutes), and finally burdock (about five minutes). When vegetables cool, mix bok choy leaves and stems with a little *ume* vinegar. Mix carrot with burdock and a little *ume* vinegar. Mix onion with green onion and a little *ume* vinegar. Place mounds on platter to serve.

Salade de Legumes avec Vinaigrette Bonne Femme (French Boiled Salad with Housewife's Dressing)

Serves 6

Vinaigrette Bonne Femme is a French mustard vinaigrette dressing. Westbrae Dijon style mustard contains the white wine which distinguishes this kind of mustard, without the acidic and tartaric acids that are added to some standard brands (even Grey Poupon).

  2 medium carrots
  2 medium turnips
  1 small cauliflower
  1 small bunch broccoli
  ½ pound green peas (¾ cup shelled) or
      green beans, in season only
  2 quarts water
  1 teaspoon sea salt
  ¼ cup *Vinaigrette Bonne Femme*

Vinaigrette Bonne Femme:

Makes ¼ cup

  3 tablespoons olive oil
  1 tablespoon wine vinegar (or rice or cider
      vinegar, or lemon juice)
  1 teaspoon Dijon mustard
  1 teaspoon red onion, minced

Cut carrot, cauliflower, and broccoli in one-and-a-half-inch lengths crosswise, then in quarter-inch strips from top to bottom, leaving flowerettes intact. Cut turnips in quarters, then in quarter-inch slices and cut green beans in one-and-a-half-inch lengths.

Bring salted water to boil, add carrots, return to boil and cook five minutes, then add other vegetables, return to boil and cook five minutes more. Drain vegetables and set aside to cool while you prepare the vinaigrette.

To prepare dressing, simply mix ingredients well. No salt is added since vegetables were cooked in salted water.

To assemble salad, pour dressing over vegetables and mix gently to serve.

Pressed Vegetable Salads

Pressed vegetable salads are made of several vegetables (as compared with quick pickles which usually focus on one) which are sliced thin, mixed with a little good quality sea salt (or pickled plum or *shiso* leaves), and pressed with a weight for several hours. The salt and pressure draw out the liquid in the vegetables and break down the hard cellular structure. The raw taste is neutralized and the vegetables become slightly pickled. Much of their fresh, crunchy quality is retained, making this an ideal daily food for that texture. Depending on how long the vegetables are salted and pressed, fermentation occurs, developing enzymes to aid digestion further.

To make pressed vegetable salads, a bowl or a plate with a lip works well to hold the vegetables and expelled juices. A glass bowl is nice for watching the process. For pressure, put another plate on top of the vegetables and weight it down with a jar of grains or beans or a heavy stone.

A pickle press is a useful kitchen utensil. After combining and arranging the vegetable-salt combination, transfer the mixture to the pickle press container or, if the volume is small, simply combine and arrange in the press. Put the top on, lock it into place and screw down the pressure plate as far as it will go. Either way,

you'll be astonished by the large volume of liquid which comes out. If you don't measure the salt and you find that the vegetables aren't pickling, you haven't added enough salt. Pressed salads are ready to eat when the juices cover the vegetables, from one hour onward, but may be pressed longer—up to about three days.

Beautiful color combinations are part of the fun of making pressed salads. Any vegetable may be used, but you'll soon see that hard roots such as carrots, turnips, and daikon break down much more slowly than leafy greens. Cabbage is usually a staple vegetable in pressed salads, especially round and Chinese cabbage or even bok choy, all of which break down easily. Kale and mustard or collard greens break down more slowly, so I often use them for color accents, the light green offset by varying shades of dark green. A hint of red from thinly sliced radish rounds, or bright yellow from summer squash in season, adds an element of delight.

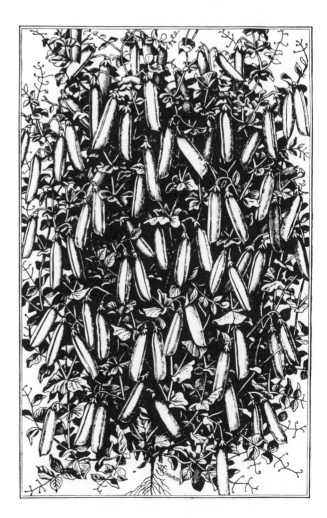

Pressed vegetable salads are usually served as is after the liquid has been poured off. Many cooks just sprinkle in salt rather than measuring, then taste the vegetables before serving to determine whether they need to be quickly run under cool water, then squeezed, to remove some salt. Don't soak the vegetables in warm water or the nutrients will be lost and the taste spoiled. However, even with the maximum amount of salt called for here—one level teaspoon per cup of vegetables, well packed—the flavor is not salty. Taste for yourself. Most of the salt comes off in the liquid, leaving a tasty vegetable you can simply fluff up and serve. For extra flavor, the same seasonings which enhance steamed or boiled vegetables may be used: *umeboshi* vinegar or rice vinegar, or lemon or lime juice, served alone or mixed with an equal part of soy sauce.

Figure about one-quarter cup of salad per serving.

Pressed Salad Number 1

Makes 1½ cups

3 cups Chinese cabbage, sliced thin and
    well packed
½ cup cucumber (green or yellow lemon
    cuke), peeled only if waxed, and sliced
    in thin quarter moons
½ cup green onion, sliced thin, or part fresh
    corn kernels or mung or soybean
    sprouts
1-4 teaspoons sea salt (or *umeboshi* or
    shiso leaves or *shiso* powder)

Rinse vegetables and pat dry. Measure and toss to evenly distribute colors. Sprinkle with salt or other seasonings and work in by rubbing over vegetables. For large amounts, layer vegetables and salt, then toss. Use less salt for overnight pressed salad (one teaspoon per quart or four cups of vegetables) and more for salads pressed for a shorter period of time. Use four teaspoons of the other seasonings in either case since their flavor is milder.

To press, place salted vegetables on a plate with a lip or in a shallow bowl. Weight down with another plate and a heavy jar, or use a salad press (available in Japanese kitchen stores) and tighten lid periodically. One-third to two-thirds of a cup of liquid comes out of these vegetables!

Pour off liquid. Discard salt water because of its strong flavor, but save liquids from other seasonings to use in cooking. Serve as is, or, to add flavor to the salt-pressed salad, sprinkle on some *umeboshi* or rice vinegar, lemon or lime juice, or one of these mixed with a little soy sauce.

Pressed Salad Number 2

Makes 2 cups

3 cups green cabbage, sliced thin and well
    packed, about ¼ head
½ cup yellow summer squash
¼ cup carrot, cut in flowers, rounds, or
    squares
¼ cup red radish
¼ cup red radish leaves
1-4 teaspoons sea salt

Slice vegetables in thin rounds and proceed as for *Pressed Salad Number 1*.

Sauerkraut Salad

Serves 6

Sauerkraut salad is the Russian people's favorite winter salad, according to a cookbook by a Russian immigrant. Because it is actually more of a pickle and therefore salty, be sure to serve small portions.

1 cup sauerkraut, drained and lightly
    squeezed
½ cup carrot, grated
½ cup green onion tops, sliced thin
1 tablespoon olive oil

To prepare, simply mix ingredients well by gently tossing.

Aspics

Aspics are gelled salads. Agar sea vegetable flakes substitute well for standard gelatin, which is made from horse or cow hooves and other bone parts. Agar flakes are easy to use. Figure two to three level tablespoons per cup liquid to be gelled, more for gels which contain other ingredients such as vegetables. Agar gelled salads firm up in about two hours at room temperature, quicker in the refrigerator. Aspics are known as *kanten* in Japan where the use of sea vegetable flakes for gelling developed.

Cucumber Aspic with Tofu Sour Cream

Serves 9

1 medium onion, chopped
1 medium cucumber, chopped
2 cups water
6 inch piece kombu sea vegetable
⅓ cup agar sea vegetable flakes
½ teaspoon sea salt
½ cup *Tofu Sour Cream*
2 tablespoons parsley, minced

Tofu Sour Cream:

Makes 2 cups

1 pound tofu, soft and fresh
2 tablespoons good quality soy sauce
2 tablespoons rice vinegar
¼ cup water or less, only if necessary for blending

Bring all ingredients to boil, except *Tofu Sour Cream* and parsley. Simmer until vegetables are soft and flakes are completely dissolved, about 8-10 minutes. Watch for foaming over upon reaching the boiling point.

Puree in hand mill or blender. Stir half the parsley into puree and pour into eight-inch square (one-and-one-half-quart) baking dish or a mold of similar size. Set to cool.

To prepare *Tofu Sour Cream*, boil whole tofu five minutes, drain, and allow to cool. Blend with other ingredients until creamy smooth, adding water last only if necessary to blend. Use a rubber spatula to press tofu down in blender.

Serve individual portions topped with a tablespoon of *Tofu Sour Cream* and a pinch of parsley.

Note: Tofu Sour Cream is the same as the *Tofu Green Goddess Dressing* recipe without the parsley.

Sesame Aspic (Kanten)

Serves 6

We experienced this artful aspic in a Japanese temple restaurant in Kyoto.

2¼ cups water
3 inch piece kombu sea vegetable
4 dried *shiitake* mushrooms
¼ cup sesame butter
¼ cup agar sea vegetable flakes
1 teaspoon good quality soy sauce
1 teaspoon Japanese horseradish paste (*wasabi*)

Bring water, kombu, and *shiitake* to boil, then simmer 10 minutes. Strain and measure to be sure you have two cups broth. Add water if necessary. Bring broth, sesame butter, and agar to boil. Stir with a wire whisk, then simmer until agar completely dissolves, about two minutes.

Aspic should be one to two inches high. A baking sheet with sides works well for large amounts.

To make *wasabi*, mix powder with water. (One tablespoon powder to one teaspoon water makes two teaspoons paste.) When preparing large amounts ahead, store in covered container so paste doesn't dry out.

To serve individual portions, cut into two-inch squares or use a cutting implement that makes a wavy line (available in kitchen stores). This was done at the temple. Spoon one-eighth teaspoon soy sauce on each serving dish, place aspic on top, and put a small dab or tiny ball of *wasabi* on top. A little *wasabi* is eaten with each bite of the aspic.

Beans and Soyfoods

More people depend upon beans as a source of complemental protein than upon any other food in the world. A variety of legumes (peas, beans, and lentils) and foods made from soybeans complement a meal of whole grains and vegetables. Beans (I'll refer to all legumes as beans since that's what everyone calls them) are known as the main protein source in a primarily vegetarian diet, although it's contained in grains, nuts, and seeds as well.

The protein in beans is made up of essential amino acids, ingredients which make protein utilization possible and some of which are lacking in grains. Just a small serving of beans, about 10 to 15 percent of the meal by volume, completes or complements the protein in grains, raising the protein utilization by about 30 percent more than if the foods were eaten separately. Corn tortillas and/or rice and black beans are a traditional grain-bean combination.

This vegetable-quality protein is superior to animal protein because it contains no saturated fat or cholesterol. Western researchers have found that dried peas and beans build up the hemoglobin content of blood much better than any other food, according to Rudolph Ballentine, M.D. (*Diet and Nutrition, a Holistic Approach,* The Himalayan International Institute, Honesdale, PA, 1979). High in carbohydrates, fiber, and the minerals calcium and iron, beans also contain vitamin A and several of the D vitamins. Beans are inexpensive and their texture and taste are luscious and satisfying. They are also good for the earth, enriching the soil as they grow.

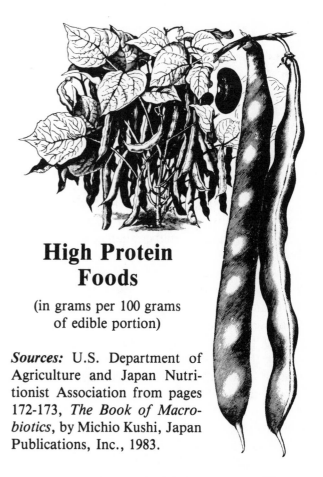

High Protein Foods

(in grams per 100 grams of edible portion)

Sources: U.S. Department of Agriculture and Japan Nutritionist Association from pages 172-173, *The Book of Macrobiotics*, by Michio Kushi, Japan Publications, Inc., 1983.

Vegetable Protein Foods

Beans

lentils	24.7
pinto beans	22.9
azuki beans	21.5
chickpeas	20.5
barley miso	14.0
soy sauce	9.0
tofu	7.8

Nuts and Seeds

pumpkin seeds 29.0
sunflower seeds 24.0
sesame seeds 18.6
almonds 18.6
walnuts 14.8
hazelnuts.............................12.6

Grains

oatmeal 14.2
wheat flour 13.3

Animal Protein Foods

cheddar cheese 25.0
fish 15-25.0
hamburger 17.9
cottage cheese........................13.6
eggs 12.9

The amount of protein in beans (and in seeds and nuts) is similar to the amount in fish and cheese, and is higher than the amount in beef or eggs.

It isn't necessary to have a bean dish at every meal. Miso and soy sauce are fermented soybean seasonings which complement grains. Because of their rich flavors and salt content (17-20 percent in soy sauce, 6-13 percent in miso), they are served in small quantities and are usually cooked into foods rather than being served as is at the table. A bowl of vegetable miso soup served with brown rice or whole wheat bread, and a lightly cooked green dish or salad, is a quick and easy meal. A plate of millet with soy sauce-seasoned cooked vegetables is another simple but well-balanced dish.

The general pattern I follow is to prepare about two pots of whole beans per week. Each pot lasts for two to three meals. I alternate the whole beans with a lunch or dinner which includes tofu or tempeh as a side dish, and a couple of meals with a simple miso soup or soy sauce broth.

Beans you buy from the bin may have stones and dirt mixed in, so be sure to sort and clean them carefully before cooking.

Beans are hard to digest for many people. Proper preparation includes a thorough soaking for at least eight hours or overnight, a change of water, boiling for five minutes with the lid off, and then pressure cooking for one hour (longer for pot cooking). Gassiness is diminished by discarding the soak water and by boiling uncovered before cooking. If an overnight soaking period doesn't seem long enough for you to digest beans, try soaking them longer, changing the water every eight hours, and then cooking them. A pressure cooker is really a wonderful utensil for grain and bean cookery. I've never had any beans clog the pressure cooker valve.

For ages in the Orient, sea vegetables (especially kombu) have been cooked along with beans to tenderize them and enhance their digestibility, as bay leaves have been used in Europe. This is a good opportunity for introducing sea vegetables into your cooking, and to unsuspecting family members who might otherwise balk at the mere idea. When the beans are cooked, the sea vegetables will completely dissolve with a stir. All the minerals from the sea vegetables are cooked in the beans, the flavor is mildly enhanced, and the seaweed is invisible. A pot of beans tastes better each time it's warmed over, so it's appropriate to enjoy them several times.

Bean sprouts are tasty, provide vitamin C and are easy to digest.

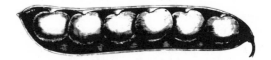

Fermented Soybean Foods

Fermented soybean foods are easier to digest than whole cooked beans. The fermentation process breaks down complex proteins and other nutrients into their simpler, more digestible forms. The fermented quality of tempeh, miso, and soy sauce, along with good quality pickles and breads, satisfies the craving for cheese and other fermented foods of animal origin. These foods are rich in digestive enzymes and bacteria which strengthen the intestines and aid in digestion. They also contain vitamin B_{12}.

Tempeh

Tempeh is a delicious fermented fresh soyfood offering a rich cheese-like flavor and meaty satisfaction. Give yourself several chances to develop your taste for this new food and it will soon become a surprising favorite. To make tempeh, whole soybeans have been well cooked and then cultured for about two days. A web grows which holds the beans together in a cake. Abundant in vitamin B_{12}, tempeh needs to be cooked through, about 10 to 20 minutes, depending on how it is cut, and is never eaten raw. Tempeh may be cooked by any technique. Try the *Baked Tempeh with Lemon-Mustard Sauce* recipe on page 78.

Miso

Miso is a fermented soybean paste. Use it like a bouillon or stock base in soups and stews or in sauces, dips, gravies, spreads, and casseroles.

To make miso, whole soybeans are cooked and mixed with mold spores *(koji)* and salt and set to age for one month to three years. During this time much enzymatic action takes place to create miso. Often a cooked grain is added to the beans to make barley *(mugi)* or brown rice *(genmai)* misos, or other, rarer kinds such as corn or buckwheat combinations. You may be fortunate enough to find small quantities of misos made with different beans such as split peas, chickpeas, or black soybeans.

The younger misos are lighter in color and sweeter in flavor than those which are aged longer. Some say the more developed misos, two to three years old, are best for creating strength and vitality. Barley miso, aged two years, is used most often in everyday macrobiotic cooking. Plain soybean *(hatcho)* miso has the strongest flavor and is usually reserved for winter cooking. The light misos are good for retaining the light color of certain dishes and soups. The best misos contain organic ingredients and good quality water and sea salt. They are naturally aged and remain unpasteurized. *Natto* miso is not used in soups, but in dressings, sauces, and spreads or as a flavor enhancer in vegetable and bean dishes. It contains soybeans, kombu sea vegetable, barley malt, ginger, and salt; the taste resembles chutney.

When miso is used daily, it acts as a blood purifier. According to *The Book of Miso* by William Shurtleff and Akiko Aoyagi (Ballantine Books or Ten Speed Press, 1983), an enzyme in miso called zybicolin is responsible for attracting to itself and expelling from the body toxic substances such as pollution, radiation, and nicotine. Miso also contains vitamin B_{12} which some people feel is difficult to get on a strictly vegetarian diet, but which occurs in all fermented foods and in sea vegetables.

Soy Sauce

Good quality soy sauce is created in much the same way as miso, but contains only soybeans, with or without the addition of a little wheat flour, and much more water. Organic ingredients, naturally aged for two to three years, are what distinguish the best soy sauces from those containing nutritionally inferior soy flakes or defatted soybean meal in place of whole beans, plus added chemicals and alcohol.

Nowadays, good quality soy sauce with wheat is often called *shoyu* and without wheat *tamari*. The misunderstanding which exists with the words tamari, shoyu, and soy sauce can be clarified with a little history.

According to the Soken Company, "It was about 1450 A.D. that Buddhist monks discovered a tasty brown liquid in the bottom of miso-making containers. They called the settling *tamari*, which means 'remains' or 'settlings' in Japanese. This thick liquid was strong and rich-tasting, adding savor and nutrition to the Japanese diet. For a while, only the nobility had access to this delightful seasoning, but through the years . . . it became an established part of the Oriental cuisine . . .

"*Shoyu* is the Japanese word for soy sauce. The word *tamari* came into popular usage in the West some 20 years ago, when George Ohsawa, a leader of the macrobiotic and natural foods movement, used it to describe natural soy sauces made in the traditional way without added chemicals. He preferred to use the word *tamari* to distinguish between extracts made over a long period of time and inferior soy sauces produced quickly in a matter of months to meet an increasing demand for *shoyu* abroad. Since then, the natural food industry has used the word *tamari* for a naturally produced *shoyu*.

" . . . Some manufacturers have debated whether or not to use the designation *tamari* for the U.S. product, because it differs from the *tamari* sold in Japan. There is no legal restriction against using the word *tamari* in the United States, however there is a group in the United States that strongly advocates not using the term . . . to avoid the confusion with the product *tamari*, the darker, thicker liquid."

Another account sheds more light on the subject. As told in the September 1984 *East West Journal* (17 Station Street, Box 1200, Brookline MA 02147), Lima Ohsawa, wife of George, says that when he gave a lecture in West Germany in 1958, a young man who ran an organic living school was eager to find out more about macrobiotics. After tasting soy sauce, *shoyu*, the man registered the name as his own trademark and brand name so only he could sell it under this name. So the Ohsawas decided to call all *shoyu tamari*.

I agree with this summary of the situation. As you see, I have used the term "good quality soy sauce" throughout this book. Of course, *tamari* may be substituted. It is wheat-free, thicker, and more expensive than soy sauce.

al dishes usually containing rich ingredients, such as a creamy Italian sauce or French quiche.

Have fun with the recipes here, but remember that tofu is not a whole food, so although it's easy to use, it shouldn't be used exclusively as many vegetarians tend to do. Tofu is not a fermented food although some people call it "soy cheese." It's made from soaked soybeans which are blended with water and strained. The white liquid is soymilk which is used as is or coagulated to make soybean curd—tofu. The mash, called *okara* in Japan, may be used in side dishes, burgers and muffins, or used for compost.

The best tofu is freshly made from organic ingredients. The water surrounding the tofu should be changed every other day for freshness. Use tofu soon after purchasing for the best flavor. The tofu that comes in vacuum sealed packages should be rinsed and transferred to a bowl of water, which should also be changed on a regular basis. According to *The Book of Tofu* by William Shurtleff and Akiko Aoyagi (Ballantine Books or Ten Speed Press, 1984), Japanese families historically ate one pound of tofu per person per week. I usually figure one pound serves six to eight. It should be cooked briefly before eating since much of it is made from uncooked beans which are made into soymilk and then cooked very briefly. Cooking also sanitizes and freshens tofu which has been sitting in a tub of water for some time.

Tofu and Soymilk

Tofu

Tofu is the saving grace for people who choose not to eat dairy foods (cheese, milk, and ice cream) and egg-based foods such as mayonnaise, but who want to create attractive and delicious main dishes, sauces, dressings, dips, and desserts which are rich and creamy and white.

Tofu helps satisfy the craving for dairy foods. Tofu's mild manner takes on the flavor of the foods it's combined with. Its texture may be made chunky or creamy. It shines in international-

Soymilk

Soymilk is made from soaked soybeans which are blended with water and strained. The white liquid which results is soymilk. Soymilk is a good alternative to cow's milk when poured over hot or cold morning cereals or in vanilla custard (see *Carmel Custard [Flan]* recipe, page 90) or rice pudding. However, because its protein content is so much higher than mother's milk and the calcium content much lower, soymilk is not the perfect food for infants or children. A grain-bean-seed milk made from ingredients cooked with a lot of water and strained or pureed is the most balanced food, next to breast milk.

No-Soak Small Bean Recipe

Serves about 8
Makes 4 cups lentils, 5½ cups azukis

2 cups split peas, lentils, azuki or
    mung beans
4 cups water
6 inch piece kombu sea vegetable
    Land vegetables (optional)
2-4 tablespoons good quality soy sauce or
    miso, or 1-2 teaspoon sea salt
    Parsley, chives, or green onion tops,
    minced for garnish

No soaking is necessary for these small beans. Place beans and water in pressure cooker, add sea vegetable, and pressure cook for one-half hour for split peas, 45 minutes for lentils, and one hour for azuki or mung beans. No flame spreader necessary. Or pot cook until done, adding water when necessary. When pressure subsides, add vegetables if included, and cook until done, then add soy sauce or miso dissolved in a little hot bean broth and simmer very gently three minutes more. For a saucier consistency, stir vigorously with a wire whisk before adding vegetables.

Figure one cup dry beans serves at least four.

To double this recipe, use one-half cup less water to cook beans, i.e. seven and one-half cups. For larger amounts, add water to two inches above beans (instead of calculating quantity by multiplying, which would result in too much water and mushy beans).

How to Cook Large Beans

Makes 4½-5¼ cups

2 cups chickpeas, black beans, pinto beans,
    etc.
8 cups water (4 cups to soak, 4 cups to
    cook)
6 inch piece kombu sea vegetable
2-4 tablespoons good quality soy sauce or
    1-2 teaspoons sea salt

Optional additions (if not making hummus):
½ cup parsley, minced
2 teaspoons savory

Rinse and soak beans at least eight hours or overnight in four cups water. Drain and reserve soak water for house plants or garden. Add four cups fresh water. Bring to boil in pressure cooker and boil vigorously uncovered five minutes to allow initial gas to escape in the form of bubbles or foam. Add sea vegetable and pressure cook one hour over medium-low heat. No flame spreader necessary. Or boil beans until done (up to three hours) adding water if necessary. Add soy sauce or salt and cook several minutes longer.

For a saucier consistency with a richer flavor, as for a stew, stir vigorously with a wire whisk, then add other ingredients and simmer uncovered until proper consistency is reached, about 15 minutes. Mix in parsley just before serving.

To double this recipe, use two cups less water to cook beans, i.e. six cups. For larger amounts, add cooking water to just two inches above beans.

Chickpea Spread or Dip (Hummus)

Serves 4-8
Makes 2 cups

This Middle Eastern dish is also written *Hoummous* or *Hommos bithine*. *Hummus* is the Arabic word for chickpeas (garbanzo beans). During Lent, Orthodox Christian communities use it to replace meat, eggs, milk, and cheese dishes. Made into a spread or dip, *hummus* is traditionally served with wedges of *pita* pocket bread, and now with any whole grain bread or breadsticks, crackers, rice cakes, chips, or vegetables. At a summer camp picnic by the river, we spread it on bread and rice cakes with a lettuce leaf underneath and alfalfa sprouts on top. A great dish for public gatherings such as pot lucks, open houses, or fairs, it's always a hit. *Hummus* also makes a delicious salad served with lettuce, lemon wedges, and very thinly sliced red onion rings. It's traditionally presented with olive oil floating on top. However, I usually forego this fatty practice except when I fix it for my father who, since his days in Persia, will eat it no other way.

    2 cups cooked garbanzo beans (see previous
        page), drained
    2 tablespoons onion, chopped
    2 cloves garlic
    2 tablespoons lemon juice
    2 tablespoons good quality soy sauce
    2 tablespoons sesame tahini
      Up to ½ cup bean cooking broth,
        to blend
    1 tablespoon parsley, minced for garnish

Blend ingredients until smooth, then garnish with parsley.

Pinto Beans and Hominy

Serves 6

A Hopi Indian dish. I've added the sea vegetable for its beneficial qualities.

2½ cups cooked pinto beans
    1 cup hominy (see page 41)
    1 teaspoon sea salt

Follow *Basic Large Beans* recipe on preceding page to cook beans. Add hominy and salt to beans and simmer until saucy, about one-half hour.

Boston Baked Beans

Serves 8

The bean pot is an American tradition. Our ancestors knew beans weren't really done until they had cooked for many hours over the hearth. Today they are still even more saucy and delicious the day after being prepared.

Baking is a wonderful way to cook them, especially in the wintertime. Notice the steady simmering when you check the beans. With heat surrounding the pot there is no chance of the bottom burning. The stove keeps the kitchen toasty and cozy on otherwise chilly days or nights. Use the time and energy to bake other foods at the same time—brown rice, a casserole, bread, a harvest vegetable pie, a week's store of toasted seeds, or a winter fruit dessert.

Navy or pea beans are used historically in this dish. Malted grain syrup is a nice substitute for brown or white sugar or molasses. Some people prefer to use apple butter. We've removed the salt pork and cut the cooking time down from six hours to one-and-one-half by presoaking the beans. Garlic, mustard, and sweetener are optional and can be eliminated or added after serving people using diet to restore their health.

    2 cups navy beans
    8 cups water (4 cups to soak, 4 cups
        to cook)
    6 inch piece kombu sea vegetable
    1 carrot, diced
    1 onion, diced
    2 large cloves garlic, sliced
    1 tablespoon dry mustard powder, or
        to taste
    2 tablespoons malted grain syrup, or to taste
    2 teaspoons sea salt

Soak beans at least eight hours or overnight in four cups water, drain, and place in ovenproof pot with four cups fresh water. Bring to boil on top of stove and cook five minutes uncovered. Add sea vegetable, cover and place in 350 degree oven to bake for one hour.

Remove sea vegetable, dice, and return to pot with remaining ingredients. Add a bit more water, about one-half to one cup, at this time if a more saucy consistency is desired. Stir well and bake one-half hour more.

Soyfood Recipes with Tofu, Soymilk or Tempeh

Summer's Mixed Vegetable Quiche

Serves 8

A really beautiful main dish pie, this quiche recipe should inspire many other possible creations. Add a little dill weed for flavor variation.

Filling:
½ cup carrot, diced small
½ cup peas, freshly shucked
½ cup green beans, cut in ¼ inch slices
½ cup fresh corn kernels
1 pound tofu, soft and fresh
¼ cup vegetable cooking broth
1 tablespoon light miso
1 tablespoon *ume* vinegar
¼ teaspoon paprika for garnish

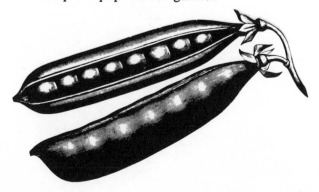

Cornmeal Crust:
⅔ cup whole wheat pastry flour
⅓ cup cornmeal or corn flour
⅓ cup water
1 tablespoon corn oil
⅛ teaspoon sea salt

Place all vegetables in steamer and steam until crisp-tender, about 10 minutes.

To prepare crust, heat together water, oil and salt in small saucepan. Mix flours well, then add water mixture and form dough.

Place cooking broth, miso, and *ume* vinegar in blender, then tofu on top. Blend until creamy smooth. Add to vegetables in bowl and stir well.

Roll out dough, transfer to corn-oiled pie pan, and form edges. Spoon in filling, dust surface with paprika, and bake at 350 degrees for one-half hour. Can be served immediately or later.

Tofu Egg Foo Young

Serves 2-4
Makes 4

Thanks to Susanne Liberty.

Patties:
½ pound tofu
¼ cup mung or soybean sprouts, firmly packed
1 green onion, sliced
2 fresh mushrooms, chopped
1 tablespoon good quality soy sauce
Sesame oil

Sauce:
½ tablespoon barley or brown rice miso
½ cup cool water
1 teaspoon brown rice vinegar
1 level tablespoon *kuzu* root starch
6 snow peas, veins removed and peas cut in ½ inch diagonals, or 2 tablespoons fresh peas.

To prepare patties, cut tofu in one-inch slices and press for five minutes to draw out excess water. A plate with a jar of beans on top works well as a weight. Meanwhile, rinse and drain sprouts. Mash tofu and mix well with other patty ingredients. Brush a baking sheet with sesame oil and shape tofu mixture into four large patties. Place on sheet to bake at 350 degrees for 40 minutes, turning patties after one-half hour.

Prepare sauce just before ready to serve.

Mix ingredients in saucepan with wire whisk and bring to boil over medium-high heat. Stir often to keep *kuzu* from lumping. A clear, shiny sauce forms in about two minutes.

To serve, place patties on serving platter and pour sauce over.

Baked Tempeh with Lemon-Mustard Sauce

Serves 4

8 ounce package tempeh
Sesame oil

Lemon-Mustard Sauce:
Makes a little more than ½ cup
½ cup cool water
1 tablespoon light miso
½ tablespoon lemon juice
½ tablespoon wet mustard
1 level tablespoon *kuzu* root starch
½ teaspoon parsley, green onion tops, or chives, minced for garnish

Cut tempeh through the center so you have two thin slabs. Cut each slab in six equal portions. Place on sesame-oiled pie pan or baking sheet to bake at 350 degrees for 20 minutes.

Place all sauce ingredients, except garnish, in saucepan and stir with wire whisk to mix thoroughly. Turn heat high and stir as mixture cooks so *kuzu* doesn't lump. When mixture comes to boil, in about two minutes, turn flame low and continue to stir about one minute more as sauce becomes clear and shiny.

To serve, pour sauce over tempeh on serving dish and garnish.

The sauce takes the place of a miso soup at a meal.

Sauces, Spreads, Dressings, Dips, and Gravies

Savory or sweet toppings make the difference between a simple meal and a great simple meal. Whole grains and pasta, vegetables, beans, casseroles and pot pies, salads, breads and crackers — all come to life with a sauce, spread, dressing, dip, or gravy. How many people would eat salad without a dressing? And what goes into most popular commercial dressings? . . . a lot of oil, salt, and natural and synthetic seasonings, not to mention additives. Good natural foods restaurants often serve brown rice or whole grain noodles with a sauce of the day. But the sauces that are part of most restaurant or packaged vegetable dishes and casseroles are usually based on rich, fatty ingredients such as butter or cream.

Wonderful toppings can be made without these ingredients. With an understanding of some basic methods of substitution, it becomes fun to create more healthful, even tastier versions.

Topping ingredients can serve several purposes depending on the amount of liquid used. Some liquid dressings (such as a vinegar or citrus-soy sauce combination) serve as marinades on their own. More creamy tofu- and nut butter-based sauces, dressings, and gravies may be used as dips or spreads when made with less water.

Figure about one-and-one-half tablespoons strong-flavored, liquid-type toppings such as Lemon-Soy, or one-quarter cup creamy type toppings per serving. When using herbs, figure twice the amount of fresh herbs as dry; crush dry herbs by hand or with a mortar and pestle or rolling pin before use.

Toppings can be divided into several categories. (See the salad section for information on particular dressing ingredients.)

- **Light Vinegar (or Citrus) and Soy Sauce (or Miso) Based Dressings.**

- **Pickled Plum *(Umeboshi)* Based Dressings**

Umeboshi are plums which are picked green and pickled with salt and a red leaf called *shiso*, according to Japanese tradition. In addition to greatly enhancing the flavor and color of foods with which they are prepared (they are bright pinkish-red in color), *umeboshi* have health-giving qualities as well. Their alkaline nature is known to neutralize an acid condition in the body. Their beneficial bacteria are said to prevent infection and help the body restore its appetite and strength in times of illness. Used in cooking they taste delicious and are known (from personal experience as well as in published literature) to help alleviate bothersome conditions ranging from a hangover to the common cold and even dysentery. Because of the salt in *ume*, a little goes a long way. Your taste will tell you.

- **Seed- or Nut Butter-Based Dressings and Spreads**

- **Kuzu Root Starch Thickened Sauces**

Kuzu is the Japanese name for a wholesome, tasteless, and colorless thickening agent used instead of cornstarch or arrowroot starch. Cornstarch is a highly refined, chemically processed product; arrowroot derives from a tropical (West Indies) tuber. Soothing and easy to digest, *kuzu* has been used over the centuries to alleviate intestinal problems. Although it is produced only in Japan at this time, there is both a source and a market for it in the United States. Its chunky texture makes it hard to measure in small amounts, but it is easily pounded into smaller pieces. *Kuzu* must be dissolved in a cool liquid before being boiled to thicken.

• **Vegetable-Based Sauces**

The three vegetable puree sauces in this book replace ethnic recipes based on tomato sauce. Since tomatoes contain solanine, a toxic substance linked to arthritis and other joint diseases (see *The Nightshades and Health* by Norman F. Childers and Gerard M. Russo, Horticultural Publications, Somerset Press, Inc., Somerville, NJ 08876), and due to their very short growing season in temperate climates, they are not usually consumed year-round or often in the macrobiotic diet. Most of the people I have served these sauces to have never even sensed they weren't eating tomatoes, until they asked why I was cooking with them! Of course there is a difference between a carrot-beet sauce and a tomato sauce, but it's close.

Another vegetable puree which makes excellent spreads utilizes winter squash. Vegetable or fruit "butters" such as onion butter or apple butter make good spreads as well.

• **Tofu- and Whole Bean-Based Sauces, Dressings, Spreads or Patés, and Dips.** See the bean section for more information on tofu and its sensual nature in sauces.

• **Whole grain flours** are traditionally used as thickening agents for gravies and sauces, from the Béchamel sauce of France to the country gravy served with biscuits in the early days of this country and today in the southeastern United States. None are included in this book, however.

NOTE: Most of the topping recipes in this book may be found in other sections of the book, along with the dish they complement. See the sauce heading in the index.

Kuzu Root Starch Thickened Sauces

Shiitake Mushroom Sauce

Makes 1 cup

1¼ cups water
1 heaping tablespoon (2 level tablespoons) *kuzu* root starch
1½ inch piece kombu sea vegetable
2 dried *shiitake* mushrooms
1-2 tablespoons good quality soy sauce
¼ teaspoon ginger, fresh grated
1 tablespoon green onions, chives, or parsley, chopped for garnish

Dissolve *kuzu* in one-quarter cup cool water and set aside. Place one cup water, sea vegetable, and mushrooms in a small saucepan and bring to boil, then simmer 10 minutes covered. Take out sea vegetable and mushrooms. When mushrooms are cool, cut into thin slices, removing and discarding hard stems. Return mushroom slices to pot with remaining ingredients and dissolved *kuzu*, and stir over high flame until mixture becomes thick, clear, and shiny, about two minutes. Garnish to serve.

Dulse-Onion Sauce

Makes 2½ cups

2 cups water
¼ cup dulse sea vegetable
1 small onion, diced
2-4 tablespoons good quality soy sauce or miso
2 heaping tablespoons (¼ cup) *kuzu* root starch
1 tablespoon parsley or chives, minced

Place *kuzu*, soy sauce or miso, and parsley or chives in one-half cup of the water. Place dulse in saucepan with remaining water and onion. Boil until onion is soft, about five minutes. Stir *kuzu* mixture and add to pot, stirring constantly until sauce becomes thick, clear, and shiny, about one minute.

Sunflower Sage Spread and Gravy

Makes 1 cup spread or 1½ cups gravy

Great on bread or crackers as a spread, or over rice as gravy. Many say it tastes like sausages or a meat gravy. Watch the rice disappear!

- ¾ cup sunflower butter
- 6 tablespoons water
- 2 tablespoons good quality soy sauce or soybean *(hatcho)* miso
- 2 teaspoons fresh sage, minced, or 1 teaspoon dry, crushed

If sunflower butter has separated, stir well. Mix ingredients in saucepan with a wire whisk and bring to boil. Turn flame low to simmer, uncovered, until heated through and smooth in texture, about two minutes.

For large amounts, figure two tablespoons per serving as a spread or one-quarter cup per serving as gravy.

Variation for Gravy:
Add:
- ½ cup water
- 1 tablespoon good quality soy sauce
  Green onion tops or parsley, minced for garnish

Pickles

Hunger is the best pickle.
—Benjamin Franklin

Long-lived cultures around the world eat fermented foods often, attributing good health to this habit. Since we are focusing on vegetable-quality foods, pickles are a good way to reap the benefits of fermentation without the fat and possible toxins in fermented animal food such as cheese.

In old times throughout the world, pickles were put up in the summer for consumption during the cold winter seasons when food supplies were short, or, more recently, just to add zip to late winter meals.

The dictionary definition of pickle is "a food preserved in a brine or vinegar solution." However, vegetables which are simply mixed with vinegar and spices and canned do not benefit from the aging process and are not considered fermented foods, but simply relishes, defined as "a highly seasoned sauce (as of pickles) eaten with other food to add flavor."

Macrobiotics broadens our perspective on pickles by introducing an array of traditional pickle varieties which have been enjoyed in the Orient for thousands of years. The art of pickling vegetables was mastered long ago in Japan where they are an indispensable finish to a traditional meal, and often enjoyed simply as hors d'oeuvres with tea or sake. Most common are various types of *takuan*, the long white radish, called *daikon*, pickled in salt and rice bran. Vegetables pickled in miso or soy sauce mash are delicious side dishes. When purchased from reliable stores or made at home, pickles are free of synthetic additives commonly found in Oriental grocery brands.

According to the founders of the Institute of Fermented Foods in Rutherfordton, North Carolina (from the article "The Daikon Difference," copyright 1984 *East West Journal*): "Lactic acid fermentation is one of nature's safest and oldest ways of preserving food. The key to good pickling is the early establishment of lactic acid-forming bacteria before undesirable bacteria have a chance to multiply. The latter, which can spoil pickling vegetables, cannot tolerate the high acidity produced by lactic acid bacteria. You can help establish these beneficial bacteria by keeping pickles cool (40-65 degrees F.), using enough salt, and mixing it thoroughly, keeping the oxygen content low by using a heavy pressing rock, and by cleaning the vegetables and utensils well."

Fermentation enhances food quality. Raw vegetables are transformed to a more assimilable form. Fermented foods activate digestion so loss of appetite doesn't occur, and thus are good for restoring health. They are an important source of vitamin B_{12} which is found in pickles as well as miso, soy sauce, tempeh, and the pickled plum.

When pickles are eaten daily, they help to establish or refurbish beneficial bacteria in our intestines, thus enabling us to assimilate the nutrients in a grain-and-vegetable-centered diet. This intestinal flora is often diminished by the acid properties of a diet high in meat and sugar.

Pickles are refreshing eaten with or after a meal in very small portions, perhaps one to three thin slices of salt bran, miso, or soy sauce mash pickles, or two tablespoons of quick pressed pickles.

Homemade Quick Pickles

Any vegetable, root or leafy green, can be pickled, but here are some favorites: Chinese and round cabbages, daikon or red radish, carrot, turnip, and cucumber. Quick pickles are usually made with just one vegetable. The vegetable is sliced thin, mixed with salt (or with the *umeboshi* or *shiso* leaves), and pressed with a weight for several hours. As with pressed vegetable salads (see pages 67 and 68), the suggested amount of salt is one teaspoon per cup of vegetables. Rub the salt into the vegetables with your fingers. The salt and pressure draw out the liquid in the vegetables, creating the pickle brine. They break down the hard cellular structure, so the raw taste is neutralized and the vegetables become more digestible. Quick pickles are ready after the vegetables are completely submerged in their own juices, in about one to three hours, although they may be pickled longer. Stored in a cool, dark place, these pickles keep for about one week. Figure two tablespoons per serving.

To make quick pickles, a plate with a lip or a shallow or regular bowl work well to hold the vegetables and the juices which come out. A glass bowl is nice for watching the process. For pressure, put another plate on top of the vegetables and weight it down with a jar of grains or beans or a heavy stone, whatever you have on hand.

Or buy a pickle press, and after combining the vegetables and salt, transfer the mixture to the pickle press container. (If the volume is small, mix the ingredients right in the press.) Put the top on, lock it into place, and screw down the pressure plate as far as it will go.

Caraway Cabbage Pickles

Makes 3 cups

These pickles develop the taste of a very mild sauerkraut.

8 cups green cabbage, thinly sliced and well packed
3 tablespoons sea salt (1 teaspoon per cup)
1 teaspoon caraway seeds

Mix ingredients well and press according to directions at left. Drain and separate somewhat to serve.

Quick Chinese Turnip Pickles

Makes 1½ cups

2 cups turnip, about 1 medium turnip
2 teaspoons sea salt
4 sprigs fresh Chinese parsley (also known as coriander or cilantro) *or* ¼ teaspoon powdered coriander
2 green onions

Cut turnip vertically in eighth-inch slices, then across in eighth-inch or half-inch slices. For variety, the larger size makes a semi-rectangular shape. Chop Chinese parsley and green onion fine and mix with turnips and salt. Press for at least three hours and serve when raw taste changes to slightly sweet.

Red Radish Ume Pickles

Makes 1 cup

Umeboshi is used here in place of salt for flavor and color variation. A beautiful pickle, bright red and pink. More plum than salt is called for in pickling: two tablespoons per cup of vegetables for quick, three hour pickles; or one tablespoon per cup for longer pickling, at least seven hours.

    2 cups red radish, root cut in thin rounds,
        greens (optional) sliced thin
    2-4 tablespoons *umeboshi* paste

Use radish greens only if they are fresh and bright green in color.

Mix ingredients well and press three hours or longer.

Other
(Store-bought)

Sauerkraut

2,200 years ago in ancient China, the first sauerkraut was prepared when rice wine was added to cabbage to preserve it for use in the winter. It was served to laborers working on the Great Wall, either raw or lightly heated through to retain its full flavor. The Tartars overran China and brought kraut back to Europe where the Germans added salt. Captain Cook's crew cured scurvy by eating sauerkraut because of its high vitamin C content. Nowadays, shredded cabbage is layered with salt and when one-fifth percent lactic acid is reached, it is declared kraut.

Sauerkraut is a splendid way to satisfy the sour taste. See the *Sauerkraut Salad* recipe on page 68. Cooking renders sauerkraut mild in flavor.

Cucumber Dill Pickles

Memories come to mind of the old pickle crock in the New Hampshire Country Store—simply-made pickles from small, firm, crisp cukes, whole dill sprigs, garlic cloves, and the salt water brine. The ingredients of good quality dills are the same as kosher dills, but are quite different from other commercial varieties which now contain vinegar, spices, and an array of chemical additives (preservatives and artificial colors).

Daikon Radish Pickles

The next three pickles focus on the long and large Japanese radish called *daikon*—meaning great root in Japanese. Daikon often weighs three to five pounds and measures 18 inches long. Many people now grow them in this country and make their own pickles. For recipes, see the *East West Journal* article mentioned earlier in this chapter and other macrobiotic cookbooks, as well as the following.

Daikon Radish and Carrot Miso Pickles

Daikon radish and carrot are sliced in half lengthwise and immersed in barley miso to be aged for six months. The package contains the vegetables coated with the miso mash. Cut off a piece of the vegetable, rinse under cool water to remove miso, and slice thin to serve. Once the package is open, it should be kept in a cool place.

To make quick miso pickles at home, ready in 24 hours, slice vegetables in quarter-inch thin rounds and press into a small bowl of miso. Rinse vegetables quickly under cool water and cut each round in four small slices to serve. Long-term pickles may be left in miso whole or cut in larger sections and stored this way for up to two years. Really delicious! Even newcomers enjoy them.

The miso used in pickling should be used soon in soup or vegetable dishes since it becomes more watery as the liquid in the raw vegetables is pulled out by the salt. Traditionally, the whole vegetables are first pickled in salt, to pull out excess liquid, and then pickled in the miso.

Daikon Radish Soy Sauce Mash Pickles

This pickle is dark in color and has a strong, full flavor. Radishes are dried in the sun and then pickled in soy sauce mash called *moromi* for one year.

Daikon Radish Rice Bran Pickles *(Takuan)*

Daikon radish rice bran pickles, called *takuan* in Japanese, were developed by vegetarian monks during Japan's feudal period. The samurai, well known for their physical, mental, and spiritual strength, included takuan in their simple diet.

According to The Institute of Fermented Foods, ". . . takuan are a rich source of B vitamins (author's note: which transfer from the rice bran into the vegetables during aging) as well as microorganisms which, in the small and large intestines, aid digestion, synthesize vitamins, and inhibit the growth of undesirable bacteria. Rice bran (called *nuka* in Japanese), the main ingredient of takuan, is particularly high in thiamine and niacin . . . In contrast, salt-pickled daikon contained an insignificant amount of this important B vitamin.

"Takuan also contain large amounts of lactobacilli bacteria which are an important link in the digestion of grains and vegetables. Scientific research has shown that these 'friendly' bacteria survive the trip through the stomach to the small intestine where they aid pancreatic enzymes in the digestion of dextrin (a carbohydrate found in grains) into simpler sugars which can be readily utilized by the body . . . Although a grain-based vegetarian diet encourages the growth of essential intestinal bacteria, they can be destroyed by improper eating habits and antibiotic therapy. It is wise, therefore, to include lactobacilli-rich foods in your diet regularly . . ."

The best daikon rice bran pickles are made at home or bought from reliable sources. Those in Oriental food stores contain a yellow dye and sometimes sugar, and are either pasteurized or contain preservatives. Pasteurization destroys microorganisms and most of the heat-sensitive enzymes.

The best quality imported takuan are made in the following ways:

Whole daikon radishes are washed, then sun-dried for about 20 days. They are then packed into large wooden kegs with a mixture of rice bran and sea salt, and weighted with a lid and heavy stones. They are left to pickle for a few months for light amber-colored, sweet and juicy pickles, or for up to one year. The pickles are then washed, pasteurized, and vacuum packed.

The other takuan, called *tsubezuke takuan*, are made in a similar manner, but aged longer, up to three years in earthenware crocks, and subsequently dried. They are rich brown in color and strong in flavor, with a chewy, dense texture. They are neither pasteurized nor vacuum packed.

Desserts

Who doesn't enjoy dessert? The sweet taste is as important as the others—salty, bitter, sour, and pungent/hot. The source of sweetness may be as diverse as winter squash, carrots or onions, or, more subtle yet, whole grain cereals. All these foods are made up of complex carbohydrates or sugars, the kind that break down over time into simpler forms, giving the body sustained energy all the while.

Many of us have lost our appreciation for these foods, having been brought up on a diet of refined and processed foods. But both taste and appetite can be resensitized and reeducated as our overstimulated bodies become more balanced. The less we eat of extreme foods such as eggs, meat, and hard, salty cheeses at one end of the spectrum, and sugar, alcohol, and drugs at the other—meanwhile introducing a wide variety of whole grains, vegetables, beans, seeds, nuts, and fruits—the more appreciation we gain for the "new" foods.

But change is best made gradually for most people. A good place to start to reestablish appreciation for the true sweet taste is with good quality desserts.

At summer camp, we serve desserts daily, usually after dinner, or at picnic outings where melon seems just right on a hot afternoon by the river. Most of the following dessert recipes can be prepared year-round. It is my hope that once you've followed the procedures involved in each recipe, you'll see possibilities for using them to create others.

No eggs, dairy products, or chemical leavening agents are included in these dessert recipes. Unrefined corn oil tastes the most like butter, so we use it in small portions for the richness it imparts (although other oils work well, too). Fruit and fruit juices, concentrated sweeteners such as malted grain and maple syrups, nuts, seeds, and minimal amounts of real sea salt and seasonings round out the ingredients. It's surprising that simple recipes using only the finest quality natural items can taste so good.

In designing dessert recipes and then working them out in the kitchen, I've come upon a few guidelines. When adding oil, I plan on one tablespoon of corn oil per cup of flour in pastries, just as in crackers and other quick breads. This is much less than you'll find elsewhere—many desserts call for equal parts oil and sweetener and no other liquid! You just don't need that much fat and sugar to make great desserts. Use apple juice or water as the basic liquid along with the oil and sweetener. I usually figure up to two tablespoons of sweetener per cup of flour. Over time, you'll find that many desserts taste fine with juice alone and no sweetener.

All the dessert recipes work well for large amounts by simply increasing ingredients.

Fruit Desserts

Melon Slice with Berry-Mint Sprig Garnish

To prepare garnish, break off two adjoining mint leaves held together with a little of the stem. Press them into melon at one end. Place one berry on either side of mint leaves. Bright red raspberries are sensational here.

Fresh Fruit Salad with Apple-Cinnamon Sauce

Serves 4
Makes 4 cups

3 cups assorted melon balls (watermelon, cantaloupe, honeydew, crenshaw, casaba, etc.)
½ cup peaches (or nectarines or apples), cut in one inch cubes
½ cup cherries (pitted), berries, or grapes, depending on season

Apple-Cinnamon Sauce:

Makes 1 cup

¾ cup apple juice
¼ cup water
⅛ teaspoon cinnamon
1 heaping tablespoon (2 level tablespoons) *kuzu* root starch

Prepare fruit close to serving time. Mix gently and place in individual serving bowls.

To prepare sauce, place all ingredients in saucepan, mix well, and bring to boil over medium flame, stirring constantly to avoid lumping. Just as boiling occurs, mixture turns into a clear, shiny sauce. Allow to cool somewhat before pouring over fruit.

Poached Pears in Cherry Sauce

Serves 4

This dessert is especially striking served on a white plate. Bosc pears taste the sweetest.

4 small bosc pears (or other variety)
1 cup cherry-apple juice or cider
½ cup water
1 tablespoon lemon juice
1 teaspoon ginger juice, fresh-grated and squeezed
⅛ teaspoon sea salt
1 heaping tablespoon *kuzu* root starch
2 tablespoons cool water
Fresh mint leaves or violet flowers for garnish (optional)

Poach whole pears with their stems on in covered pan with juices and water until tender, 20-45 minutes depending on hardness of pears. Baste occasionally. Remove pears to serving platter and arrange them in standing position. Cut off bottom to form flat surface for any pears that don't stand up well.

Measure liquid (amount may vary due to different cooking times) and figure one heaping tablespoon *kuzu* root powder per cup liquid. Dissolve *kuzu* in an equal amount of cool water and add to hot liquid in pan. Bring to boil, stirring constantly, while mixture becomes thick and shiny, about one minute. Pour sauce over pears so they are well covered and sauce pools to cover plate. Garnish stem to serve, warm or cool.

Fresh Grape Gel with Nutty Granola Topping

Serves 9

Thanks to Diana Jones for inspiration on this granola which is neither overly sweet nor oily. A great topping for gels, puddings, in cobblers, as a pie crust, or in cookies.

3 cups apple juice
1 cup water
¾ cup agar sea vegetable flakes
½ teaspoon sea salt
1 cup seedless grapes
1 cup *Nutty Granola* for topping

Nutty Granola:

Makes 7 cups

4 cups rolled oats (or part wheat and rye flakes, about ½ cup each)
¾ cup sunflower seeds, toasted
¼ cup sesame seeds, toasted
½ cup peanuts, toasted
½ cup almonds, toasted and chopped coarsely
¼ cup corn oil
¼ cup maple syrup
½-1 cup raisins (or currants)
1 cup water (or apple juice)
1 tablespoon vanilla
1 tablespoon cinnamon
½ teaspoon sea salt

Place first four ingredients in pot to soak for five minutes. Bring to boil over high flame, then simmer uncovered until agar completely dissolves, about five minutes. Add grapes in last minute of cooking to soften them slightly, then pour all into container to gel, about two hours at room temperature. An eight-inch square one-and-one-half quart glass baking dish works well.

To prepare topping, mix first five ingredients well. Place remaining ingredients, except vanilla, in saucepan and bring just to boil, then add vanilla, stir and pour over dry ingredients. Mix well.

Spread out on two cookie sheets (no oil necessary) and bake at 350 degrees for about one-half hour, stirring two times during cooking. Do not allow granola to get too dark. Let cool 15 minutes before using or placing in container to store.

To serve, cut gel in squares and sprinkle with topping.

Variation: For a *Cherry Gel*, substitute cherry or apple-cherry juice for apple juice and pitted cherries for grapes. The possibilities are endless.

Puddings

Caramel Custard (Flan) with Topping

Serves 9

Flan originated in Spain as a custard with a burnt sugar layer.

Custard:

   3 cups soymilk
   1 cup water
  ½ cup plus 1 tablespoon agar sea vegetable
     flakes, well packed
  ½ cup maple syrup
  ¼ cup sesame tahini
   1 teaspoon vanilla
  ¼ teaspoon sea salt

Caramel Topping:

  ¼ cup maple syrup
  ¼ cup water
   1 tablespoon agar sea vegetable flakes
     Cinnamon to dust surface

To prepare custard, place all ingredients, except soymilk and vanilla, in pot to soak for five minutes. Bring to boil, then simmer until agar completely dissolves, about 10 minutes. Stir with a wire whisk to dissolve tahini. Let cool three minutes, then add to soymilk with vanilla. Stir and strain into eight-inch square one-and-one-half quart baking dish, pressing ingredients through strainer with a rubber spatula to dissolve any small lumps. Let custard set for 15 minutes.

Prepare caramel topping by soaking ingredients, except cinnamon, in small saucepan for five minutes, then bringing to boil and simmering until agar is dissolved, about three minutes. Pour through strainer over custard so a thin layer covers the surface, and dust with cinnamon. Allow custard to gel for two hours at room temperature, then cut in squares to serve.

Baked Indian Pudding

Serves 4

This was a traditional colonial Thanksgiving dessert. How fitting when one remembers that the Native Americans saved the Pilgrims from starvation by sharing with them their native grain, corn.

The Indians probably made their version with berries for the sweet taste. The colonial recipes evolved to include molasses, sugar, lard or butter, baking soda, eggs, and milk. The pudding was baked for five to seven hours, in a well-greased stone crock. According to the colonial restaurant in Boston, Durgin-Park, baked Indian pudding had such an impact on American cuisine that it was even made by chefs in ships' galleys from Valpariso, Chile to Hong Kong.

Farther west, the traditional Hopi didn't eat desserts per se, but included sweet dishes in with the main meal on occasion. Hopi sweet corn puddings were lowered into a preheated pudding pit, covered, and the pit sealed with wet mud. The pudding baked overnight and was served warm with stew for breakfast. Sweet puddings are now served for breakfast on Indian feast and dance days, at weddings, and at naming parties for babies. Small pieces are broken off and eaten with the fingers. The leftover portion is dried, pulverized, and made into a beverage by adding hot water.

   1 cup cornmeal
  ¼ teaspoon sea salt
   3 cups water
  ½ cup raisins
  ½ teaspoon cinnamon
  ¼ cup malted grain syrup or part maple
     syrup

Place cornmeal and salt in saucepan. Add water gradually and stir to prevent lumps. A wire whisk is very helpful. Bring to boil over high flame, stirring constantly, until mixture thickens, about five minutes. Add remaining ingredients. Pour mixture into corn-oiled baking dish. Bake at 400 degrees for one hour, uncovered, stirring once halfway through so raisins don't stick on bottom. Let sit about one hour before serving.

Pies

Lemon-Lime Pudding Pie

Serves 8-10

Delicious and so simple. When designing this recipe, I noticed that oat and brown rice flours don't set up as well as wheat flour, and grain sweeteners don't taste as good alone with flour as does maple syrup, so there is a little of each kind of sweetener included here.

    1 cup whole wheat pastry flour
2½ cups water
 ¼ teaspoon sea salt
 ¼ cup brown rice syrup
 ¼ cup maple syrup
 ½ teaspoon vanilla
 1 tablespoon lemon juice
 1 tablespoon lime juice
 1 teaspoon grated lemon and/or lime rind
 ½ cup hazelnuts or pecans, toasted,
       chopped, and crushed for crust
    Cinnamon for garnish

Add cool water to flour in pan, a little at a time, stirring constantly to prevent lumping, or stir with a wire whisk. Add salt and bring to boil over high flame, stirring often. Cover pot and place flame spreader underneath to simmer for a half hour.

Sprinkle nuts over sides and bottom of small, lightly-oiled pie plate. Add remaining ingredients to pot in last few minutes of cooking.

Mix well. Pour mixture into pie plate to gel, about 1-2 hours. Sprinkle top with a pinch of cinnamon.

For large amounts, cut most pies in eight serving slices and one or two in 10 slices for children.

Variation: For a *Lemon* or *Lime Pudding Pie*, substitute two tablespoons of either citrus juice and one teaspoon of the rind.

American Berry Pie (Strawberry-Blueberry Pie)

Serves 10

The bright red and blue berries make this a very festive summer dessert that brings "oohs" and "aahs!"

Filling:
 2 pints strawberries
 1 pint blueberries
 ½ teaspoon sea salt
 ½ cup rice syrup
 ½ cup agar sea vegetable flakes
    Basic Single Pie Crust Dough

Basic Single Crust Pie Dough:
1½ cups whole wheat pastry flour
 ½ cup water
1½ tablespoons corn oil
 ¼ teaspoon sea salt

To prepare filling, rinse strawberries by placing in a bowl of cool water, swishing them quickly and removing them. Pinch off stems *after* rins-

ing or some of the flavorful juice will be lost in the water. Cut only very large berries in half. Leave others whole.

Place strawberries in saucepan and sprinkle with salt. Pour rice syrup over and sprinkle agar flakes over all. Cover pan and bring to boil, then simmer until agar is completely dissolved, around 15 minutes. Strawberries are so full of liquid (about one-half cup comes out) that no added liquid is necessary as long as you keep the flame at medium-low. Stir several times. Add blueberries in last five minutes of cooking time, after the strawberries are soft and juicy and the agar is almost dissolved. This way the blueberries become soft, but retain their round shape and distinct color and flavor.

To prepare pie dough, heat water, oil, and salt together. This mixes the ingredients well, thoroughly dissolves the salt, and makes for a smoother dough. Add warmed liquid to flour. Stir to form a kneadable dough, then knead quickly and briefly just to make dough smooth. Add more flour only if necessary. Roll dough out immediately as whole wheat pastry flour tends to harden with time, and place in corn-oiled pie pan. Crimp edges and bake at 350 degrees just until edges are barely golden, about 15 minutes. Allow to cool slightly before filling, or reserve for later use.

Pour filling into prebaked *Basic Single Crust Pie Dough.* Allow to gel, about three hours at room temperature or less in the refrigerator.

Cookies

• **The basic formula** I use for pastries (pie dough and cookies) and for crackers, breadsticks, pretzels, etc., is:

  1 tablespoon oil per cup flour
  ⅛ teaspoon sea salt per cup flour
  Liquid is about one-third volume of flour.

• **Remember to work quickly** with whole wheat pastry flour as it tends to harden if left to sit, even when covered with a damp cloth.

• **Substitute part or all maple syrup for malted grain syrup** if you want a distinctly sweet as compared to a subtly sweet cookie.

• **To make grain syrups more pourable,** heat whole jar in water (that extends about three-quarters of the way up the side of the jar), then pour contents into another saucepan with one-quarter cup water and heat to mix thoroughly. Pour this thinned version back into jar and it will remain pourable. Store in a cool place during the warm months.

Almond Cookies

Makes 2 dozen

3 cups whole wheat pastry flour, store-
    bought or fresh, finely ground
1 cup apple juice (or ⅔ cup juice, ⅓ cup
    maple syrup)
3 tablespoons corn oil
½ teaspoon sea salt
1 tablespoon almond extract
24 almonds

Heat juice, oil, and salt together. This blends ingredients well, thoroughly dissolves the salt, and
helps create a soft, smooth dough. Add extract,
stir, and add to flour to form dough. Knead
briefly until smooth. Don't let dough sit or it
tends to harden. Roll dough out to quarter-inch
thickness and cut with three-inch round cutter or
jar lid. Press a whole almond in center of each
cookie and place on corn-oiled cookie sheet.
Bake at 350 degrees until golden on bottom side,
about 12-15 minutes. Cookies harden as they
cool.

Ginger Cookies

Makes 2 dozen

3 cups whole wheat pastry flour, store-
    bought or fresh, finely ground
⅓ cup malted grain syrup (brown rice syrup)
    or maple syrup
⅔ cup apple juice
3 tablespoons corn oil
2 tablespoons ginger, fresh grated
½ teaspoon sea salt
    Raisins for garnish (optional)

Heat all ingredients together except flour and
raisins, then stir and add to flour to form dough.
Don't let dough sit or it tends to harden. Roll out
to quarter-inch thickness and cut with three-inch
round cookie cutter or other shape. With soft
dough such as this, it's easier to roll the dough
out and transfer it to the oiled sheet for cutting
so you don't spoil the shapes by moving them
from the cutting board to the sheet. These
cookies are nice pressed with a decorated
wooden mold, or press a single raisin in the
center of round cookies. Bake until golden on
bottom, 12-15 minutes at 350 degrees.

Beverages

Non- or very mildly-stimulating teas, made from twigs, stems, leaves, flowers, or roots, as well as cereal grain beverages, are drinks which may be enjoyed with none of the negative side effects of regular teas or coffee: excitability, irritability, increased blood pressure and pulse rate, stressed heart and kidneys, and the possibility that caffeine may be a cancer-causing agent. The wide variety available makes for a smooth transition to these satisfying drinks. Flavors range from mild and gentle to rich and strong depending on preparation.

Twig tea, called *kukicha* in Japanese, has been confused with green leaf tea, called *bancha*. Since most of the caffeine in tea is found in the leaves, the lower twigs used in twig tea are much preferred by health-conscious people, for that reason as well as the difference in taste. Twig teas are harvested in the fall and winter when the leaves have hardened and contain far less tannin and caffeine than leaves picked for green tea. Most people don't notice any side effects from these substances in such small amounts.

Twig Tea

All teas that are not herb teas come from the same tea plant. One of the most popular beverages among macrobiotic people is twig tea. Made from the twigs and stems, instead of the leaves, of the tea bush, it has an attractive, earthy aroma and a mellow flavor. Since it has been roasted several times to eliminate the caffeine and tannic acid-containing oils, there is no need to roast it at home. Tannic acid is what gives green and black teas their astringent quality. As a free acid, tannin coagulates protein, possibly disrupting digestion. Tannins, also present in chocolate and carob, can slow the growth rate of young animals and are not recommended for children.

Twig tea is soothing to the stomach and is known as an aid to digestion. It acts as a buffer solution to partially neutralize either an acidic or alkaline condition, and is therefore recommended after eating to help balance the possible acidity or alkalinity that may result from imbalances in a meal.

Caffeine content per 8 ounces

twig tea *(kukicha)* . . . . .18.6 mg.
green leaf tea *(bancha)* . . . . .43.8 mg.
black tea . . . . 80 mg.
coffee . . . . 117 mg.

Analysis of brewed twig and green leaf teas done by Rodale Press in Emmaus, Pennsylvania.

Since tea is one of the most heavily chemicalized crops in Japan, look for organic twig tea. While good quality twig tea is taken from bushes unsprayed and unfertilized for at least two years, the organic tea comes from bushes which have been free of chemicals for five years. The best twig teas are three-year-old teas. During this aging period a natural enzymatic action causes mellowing and improvement in flavor and aroma.

According to Ohsawa America (P.O. Box 3608, Chico, CA 95927), what is now called Ohsawa tea was created by a tea grower who was a student of the foremost teacher of macrobiotics, George Ohsawa. Ohsawa was concerned about the "extremely imbalanced yin acidity of the popular green tea the Japanese people consume the way Americans do coffee." So together they developed twig tea to be a balanced drink which was completely safe for daily consumption by adults, children, and people in a weakened condition. Ohsawa tea is different from other twig teas because of its particular balance of leaves, stems, and twigs.

It is also available in tea bags. The twigs have been ground into a powder and the bags are simply steeped in hot water.

Other Teas and Grain "Coffees"

Today, there are many other high quality teas which are made of ingredients which are domestically, and sometimes organically, grown. All are delicious and soothing year-round—served hot to thoroughly warm the soul, at room temperature, or chilled, perhaps with a hint of freshly squeezed lemon or lime, on a hot midsummer afternoon. Alfalfa and red clover teas are my favorite herb teas. Other non-stimulating varieties which have received good reviews from guests derive from wild plants such as chickweed, malva, horsetail, coltsfoot, and mullein, or domesticated comfrey, camomile, raspberry or strawberry leaves, rosehips, lemon grass, and chrysanthemum. Mint teas are mildly stimulating. Sassafras bark and *mu* tea (a combination of nine or sixteen herbs and roots) produce brews with distinct flavors. Licorice root brewed alone or with other teas is very sweet. For more variety, a simple combination of one-quarter twig tea with three-quarters of one of the above herb teas is quite satisfying.

To prepare, simply bring water to boil, turn heat off and add flowering herb or leaf tea. Figure two teaspoons dry herbs or twigs per cup of water. Stir once to moisten tea and cover to let steep five to ten minutes. For twig, bark, and root teas, simmer gently for 10 minutes to extract flavor.

Grain "teas" and "coffees" offer a great variety of alternatives to twig or non-stimulating herb teas. Twig tea with toasted brown rice, roasted corn tea, and roasted barley tea are very simple traditional beverages with delicious flavors and aromas. The Iroquois are known to have made a beverage from the roasted shells of sunflower seeds.

Cereal grain beverages, known as grain "coffees," actually contain no coffee, but do have the similar dark color, rich aromas, and flavors. Roasted barley tea differs from barley coffee. The former is made from roasted whole barley whereas barley coffee is made from barley which has been hulled, then dark-roasted and ground, coarsely for brewing or fine for instant versions.

Grain coffees are also made from roasted grains other than barley, such as rye and wheat, and sometimes contain roots such as chicory or dandelion. Two brands which I have found most satisfying to the general public are an American version called Heritage (F.L. Wilson Company, Parsons, KS 67357) made from 100 percent roasted pearled barley, one of the few coffee substitutes processed without chemical extraction; and Yannoh (also known as Ohsawa coffee), the original coffee substitute created by early proponents of macrobiotics. Japanese yannoh is a lightly-roasted blend of ground azuki beans, Japanese red peas, black soybeans, brown rice, and dandelion root. Another version, from the Lima Company in Belgium, contains barley, rye, chicory, and wild acorns.

Many people wean themselves from a lifetime habit of coffee-drinking by switching to full-strength grain coffee, then gradually lessening the strength and quantity as their tastebuds become renewed and they are able to enjoy the milder flavors. It's fun to prepare grain coffees in different ways, with a hint of another flavor such as anise seed or cinnamon for special meals, or in different strengths ranging from regular to espresso style.

For a daily brew of medium strength, use one to two level teaspoons per cup of water. For a richer, full strength "espresso coffee," figure two level teaspoons to one tablespoon per cup of water. Store teas and grain beverages in airtight containers.

Liquid Consumption

Beverages are consumed for various reasons — thirst, sociability, pleasure, to replace water lost during hard physical activity, or for a warming or cooling effect.

In the macrobiotic approach to diet, soup is frequently taken before the meal and a beverage afterward. Cooked grains contain about 60 percent water and vegetables often contain 90 percent water. Liquid is usually not taken during the meal as it may interfere with the digestive process. Liquids which are not too hot or cold are best.

One helpful maxim is: Drink when thirsty. If you're very thirsty, and you haven't been doing strenuous activity, consider that your salt intake may be creating the thirst. Too much soy sauce, miso, or *umeboshi* in cooking, using soy sauce at the table instead of in cooking, taking excessive amounts of table seasonings and pickles, and too many salty snack foods such as crackers and chips all create thirst. Other foods which may promote thirst are sweets and too high a volume of dry foods like rice cakes and other crackers, even if they are unsalted.

Twig Tea

Serves 4-8

This Japanese beverage is called *kukicha* and is often incorrectly referred to as *bancha*.

    4 cups (1 quart) water
    8 teaspoons (little less than 3 tablespoons)
        twigs

Figure two teaspoons per cup water for everyday tea. Bring water to boil, turn heat low, add twigs and cover to simmer gently 10 minutes to extract the flavor from the twigs. Twigs can be reused up to four times with a pinch of fresh tea added each time.

To prepare large amounts ahead of time, just add twigs to boiling water and turn heat off, then reheat when ready to serve.

Twig Tea with Toasted Brown Rice

Serves 4-8

4 cups (1 quart) water
4 tablespoons (¼ cup) roasted twig tea with roasted brown rice

Known as *genmai kukicha* (*genmai* means brown rice), this tea can be purchased or prepared at home. For either, figure one tablespoon per cup water as the flavor is more subtle than other teas. Bring water to boil, turn flame low and add tea. Simmer 10 minutes.

To make your own, figure equal amounts brown rice and twig tea. Rinse, then toast raw rice in dry skillet until golden and crispy, about five minutes. Mix with twigs.

DELICIOUS!

Roasted Corn Tea

Serves 4-8

This tea has a very soothing flavor and a nice blonde-amber color.

4 cups (1 quart) water
4 tablespoons (¼ cup) roasted corn

To make your own, rinse then dry roast one cup whole dry, yellow grain corn in a skillet. Kernels should become dark golden brown over a medium flame in about 15 minutes. Stir frequently to avoid scorching.

Figure one tablespoon per cup water. Bring water to boil, turn flame low and add roasted corn. Simmer 10 minutes.

Roasted Barley Tea

Serves 4-8

Known as *mugicha* (*mugi* = barley, *cha* = tea), this beverage is made with unhulled barley.

4 cups (1 quart) water
8 teaspoons (little less than 3 tablespoons) roasted barley

Figure two teaspoons per cup water. Bring water to boil, turn heat low, add barley and simmer 10 minutes.

Hominy Tea

Serves 4-8

Hominy tea is the liquid which remains after the second cooking of whole corn for hominy (see page 41).

Alfalfa, Red Clover, and other Herb Teas

Serves 4-8

4 cups (1 quart) water
8 teaspoons (little less than 3 tablespoons)
    dry herbs

Bring water to boil, turn heat off and add tea.
Stir once to moisten tea, then cover to steep 5-10
minutes.

Grain "Coffee"

Serves 4-8

4 cups (1 quart) water
4-8 teaspoons instant powder or granules
    (1-2 teaspoons per cup water)

Bring water to boil and turn flame low. For instant variety, simply add water to measured
amount powder in cup or add powder to pot for
larger amounts. For granules, add to pot gradually to avoid foaming over, cover, and simmer
very gently 10 minutes. Another method is to
add granules to cool water and bring to boil,
watching carefully to avoid foaming upon boiling. Turn flame off to steep 10 minutes.

Variations:

Espresso Style—Figure two teaspoons to
one tablespoon grain coffee per cup water.

Cinnamon "Coffee"—Prepare as espresso
style adding two six-inch sticks cinnamon,
broken in several pieces, per quart water.

Anise "Coffee"—Prepare as espresso style,
adding one tablespoon anise seed per quart
water.

Index